Reflections
THE LEGACY OF
LEE KUAN YEW

Reflections
THE LEGACY OF
LEE KUAN YEW

Editors

Yang Razali Kassim
Mushahid Ali

S. Rajaratnam School of International Studies,
Nanyang Technological University, Singapore

World Scientific

NEW JERSEY · LONDON · SINGAPORE · BEIJING · SHANGHAI · HONG KONG · TAIPEI · CHENNAI · TOKYO

Published by

World Scientific Publishing Co. Pte. Ltd.

5 Toh Tuck Link, Singapore 596224

USA office: 27 Warren Street, Suite 401-402, Hackensack, NJ 07601

UK office: 57 Shelton Street, Covent Garden, London WC2H 9HE

Library of Congress Cataloging-in-Publication Data
Reflections (Yang Razali Kassim and Mushahid Ali)
  Reflections : the legacy of Lee Kuan Yew / [edited by] Yang Razali Kassim (S. Rajaratnam School
of International Studies, Nanyang Technological University, Singapore), Mushahid Ali
(S. Rajaratnam School of International Studies, Nanyang Technological University, Singapore).
    pages cm
  Includes bibliographical references and index.
    ISBN 978-9814723886 (alk. paper) -- ISBN 9814723886 (alk. paper)
    1. Lee, Kuan Yew, 1923-2015. 2. Singapore--Politics and government. 3. Singapore--Economic
policy. 4. Singapore--Social policy. I. Yang Razali Kassim, editor. II. Mushahid Ali, 1941- editor.
III. Title.
  DS610.73.L45R45 2015
  959.57'051092--dc23
                        2015031764

British Library Cataloguing-in-Publication Data
A catalogue record for this book is available from the British Library.

In-house Editor: Karimah

Typeset by Stallion Press
Email: enquiries@stallionpress.com

Printed in Singapore

Reflections: The Legacy of Lee Kuan Yew

Contents

Foreword

Ong Keng Yong

AS WE PONDER over life after Lee Kuan Yew, the most important thing, to me, that the founding prime minister left behind is a flourishing Singapore. From a little known island, Singapore is today a prominent city–state in the global community. Most people in and outside Singapore see it as synonymous with Lee Kuan Yew and *vice versa*. Without Lee Kuan Yew, will Singapore be just as good or will it decline? Indeed, can Singapore survive Lee Kuan Yew?

I posed this question to several young Singaporean researchers at the S. Rajaratnam School of International Studies (RSIS) and they gave me a unanimous "yes". One-third of them underlined the need for adjustment in policy and political approaches by the government in the post-Lee Kuan Yew era to win support from younger Singaporeans. Singapore has changed and Lee Kuan Yew's People's Action Party (PAP) must also change to remain in power. Educational progress, technological advances and a more profound wish for the future have made electoral politics more challenging. The political leadership and the government have to deal with more complexities as compared to Lee Kuan Yew's time on the job.

I posed a second question on what is the one thing that Lee Kuan Yew bequeathed to Singaporeans. Almost all of them replied "pragmatism". To them, he embedded in the citizens of his country a belief in Singapore's vulnerabilities and ability to overcome adversity with practical solutions. Thinking about how to beat the odds and making the best of the situation with a creative way out is a hallmark of Singaporeans after five decades of PAP and Lee Kuan Yew.

The key to PAP's durability in government is the trust factor. Many Singaporeans had put their trust in Lee Kuan Yew and his team. In addition, the prevention of corruption is described as setting Singapore apart from the neighbourhood and which will continue to make Singapore attractive to investors and people wanting to make a difference in their lives as they move into the future without Lee Kuan Yew.

In my opinion, the Lee Kuan Yew software is well ingrained in Singaporeans. This covers seven habits: take the world as it is; plan for the future; solve problems quickly and creatively; do it right the first time; carry out what has been decided; focus on outcome; and ensure follow-up. Therefore, the question really is, does the next generation of leaders have the gumption and gusto to govern in the best interest of Singapore and what will determine this capability?

Lee Kuan Yew and his team delivered over the years as they played "tough and care", and shared the achievements with Singaporeans. Their successors have to find their own "mojo" to stay in charge. The style and vocabulary will be different but they should be able to deliver in their own way. ∞

Ong Keng Yong is Executive Deputy Chairman at the S. Rajaratnam School of International Studies (RSIS), Nanyang Technological University, Singapore.

Preface

Yang Razali Kassim

THE MORNING after the demise of Mr Lee Kuan Yew, the head of RSIS, Ambassador Ong Keng Yong, asked me what we planned to do to reflect this epochal event in *RSIS Commentary*, the School's primary platform for the articulation of views on major issues. Before we knew it, the response to this momentous point in Singapore's history flowed naturally. Immediately, Executive Deputy Chairman Ong reminisced on the imprint of Mr Lee on Singapore's bilateral relations with the United States, a strategic partner in Singapore's network of key bilateral ties, which appeared in the local media. Indeed, a number of current and previous members of the RSIS Board of Governors had equally been reflecting on the legacy of Mr Lee. Chairman Eddie Teo spoke to a gathering of senior civil servants in his capacity as Chairman of the Public Service Commission three days after Mr Lee's passing. Eminent scholar and former Board of Governors (BOG) member University Professor Wang Gungwu reflected on the history, heritage and the idea of Singapore. Ambassador Chan Heng Chee ruminated on her experiences with Singapore's first prime minister from her days as a critical young lecturer, while Ambassador Barry

Desker, Distinguished Fellow and former Singapore ambassador to Jakarta, recalled Mr Lee's pivotal role in rebuilding ties with Indonesia under President Suharto. Various other authors, starting from new Dean Joseph Liow to other members of the RSIS faculty as well as associates and younger researchers, likewise pondered over what it meant to have grown up under the towering shadow of Lee Kuan Yew, the founder of modern Singapore. A key take away is that within his huge legacy is the "Lee Kuan Yew software" that will remain to define the post-LKY era.

In the end, what we came out with was a series on The Legacy of Lee Kuan Yew, which we published in *RSIS Commentary* following his passing, and which we eventually put together as a coherent whole in this special issue of *Strategic Currents*, an RSIS periodical. This is not just a compilation of essays on a giant of a leader. It is a publication that will certainly be of value to future research on Singapore and the making of The Singapore Story. As scholars, researchers and journalists in the years to come look back to understand what made Singapore tick and rise from ordinariness to become an epitome of success in the modern world, they would find this edited volume difficult to ignore. In it they will find reflections on the various engaging facets of the charismatic and colourful personality that was Lee Kuan Yew, whom Chan Heng Chee aptly describes as the 'last of the era of the post-war great leaders'.

This book covers three chapters of almost 30 essays reflecting Lee Kuan Yew's leadership; his imprint on Singapore's foreign policy and diplomacy; and his legacy on nation-building, including how some from the younger generation viewed him. In short, this special issue offers the reflections on modern Singapore's founding father by an array of authors from different generations who had worked closely with, or for him, as well as grown up under him — as thinkers, scholars and researchers, each providing different perspectives on the multifaceted and impressive legacy of Singapore's first prime minister. This book will hopefully also add to the collection of publications on Lee Kuan Yew's contribution to the developing world's unending quest for development and its various models — from nation-building, statehood and leadership, to governance and the management of plural societies. ၐ

Yang Razali Kassim is a Senior Fellow and Editor, Strategic Currents & RSIS Commentary; and Editor, Reflections: The Legacy of Lee Kuan Yew, a Special Issue of Strategic Currents.

Introduction

The Charisma of Being Modern Singapore's Founding Father

Mushahid Ali

WHEN PANDIT Jawaharlal Nehru died as India's founding prime minister, a wise Singaporean observer wrote: "It was not the office of Prime Minister that made Nehru great, rather it was Nehru who made the Prime Minister's office great." Similarly it was not the premiership of Singapore that made Lee Kuan Yew great, it was Lee Kuan Yew who invested greatness to the Prime Minister's Office which he filled for 31 years.

When Lee died on 23 March 2015 aged 91, he had left the Prime Minister's Office for nigh 25 years; yet he commanded the respect and recognition of the people of Singapore as the founding father of the nation who had guided and sustained the tiny island state to greatness as among the richest countries in the world, one that had transformed its status from Third World to First within a span of a generation.

xx   *Reflections: The Legacy of Lee Kuan Yew*

The outpouring of grief and gratitude by the million and half of the population who attended his wake and lying in state, and turned out to bid farewell to his funeral procession, testified to an incredible affection for the stern father who had affirmed that he would rather be feared than loved. In the end, they acknowledged that they owed a debt of gratitude to the indefatigable leader who gave his life for the development, progress and success of Singapore.

The eulogies from all over the world testify to the universal admiration that Singapore's first prime minister enjoyed for Singapore's achievements in nation-building, physical transformation, economic development, contribution to international commerce, communications and knowledge advancement. Among his greatest contribution to Singapore's growth has been the self-confidence he instilled in the citizens that they are masters of their destiny, and that they can build a society united in their resolve to ensure their survival as a multi-cultural yet modern nation in Southeast Asia that will prosper for a century or more.

The articles in this compendium aims to capture some of the achievements and contributions of Lee Kuan Yew as founding prime minister of Singapore. It is also hoped that they will serve as signposts for its future progress and survival as a sovereign state in the Asia–Pacific region. ☙

Mushahid Ali is a Senior Fellow and Co-editor, Reflections: The Legacy of Lee Kuan Yew, a Special Issue of Strategic Currents.

Chapter I
Lee Kuan Yew's Leadership

History, Heritage and the Idea of Singapore

By Wang Gungwu

Synopsis

Lee Kuan Yew's success in transforming Singapore from a plural immigrant society into a multicultural nation rested on the core values that shaped him and the power systems that he chose to serve his political cause.

Commentary

IT IS not too early to think about Lee Kuan Yew's place in history. The sense of loss that Singaporeans demonstrated when he lay in state was genuine and deep. The eulogies from all over the world testify to the impact of his achievements in the city–state that he led.

To many leaders in Asia, what he did was to provide remarkable answers to the problems of decolonisation and nation-building that the region experienced after the end of World War Two. Some might focus on his doing this with so small a country; others wonder what more he could have done if he had more land and people under his care.

Heritage and shifting realities

His success rested on his ability to understand his environment and the transformations it was encountering. It rested on the core values that shaped him and the power systems that he studied and eventually chose to serve his political cause. The former relates to his origins as someone descended from many generations of Chinese in Southeast Asia who had lived among a variety of people and under several different kinds of regimes. The latter draws on his personal capacity to learn from history and respond to shifting realities.

Chinese society frowned on the idea of leaving home and not returning. But, for centuries, many in southern China did so when conditions were favourable, although the majority of males who settled down with their local wives and descendants were by and large assimilated. However, there was one area that was exceptional — the territories around Batavia (Jakarta) and Malacca, where the Netherlands East Asia Company encouraged enterprising Chinese to organise themselves to help the Company trade with China.

Their communities expanded on both sides of the Straits of Malacca when the British arrived at the end of the 18th and the beginning of the 19th century. The locally-evolved organisations extended their activities to the settlements in Penang and Singapore. Their members adapted to the Anglo–Dutch as well as to the Malay worlds. They understood well the characteristics of the neighbouring lands and peoples and were well-prepared to become key players in the growing trade with China.

By the end of the 19th century, their descendants were responding to the modernising changes in the region and were learning to appreciate the virtues of different kinds of political systems and the advantages of industrial capitalism.

This was also when new generations of elites in China were adjusting to the demands of Western imperial power and awakening to the need for national consciousness. They were also acquiring modern knowledge and sought the support of the Chinese overseas. This was a challenge to the distinctive Chinese communities in Southeast Asia. Did they have to choose between affirming their special relations with the Western colonial states that had been established or join their compatriots in supporting a new Chinese nation?

Making plural society a multicultural nation

Many Chinese who had long settled in the region were divided in their loyalties and remained undecided until the Japanese invasions. After 1945, it became clear that the era of Western empires was coming to an end. For most Chinese, the choice from now on was to identify with the new native nations or return to China. Only in British Malaya was there another option: the chance to make a plural society develop into a multicultural nation.

Coming from this settled Straits Chinese background, Lee Kuan Yew chose to build on that possibility. He had to do so in the midst of local nationalist hopes, a primarily

Chinese communist revolution and an Anglo–American offensive against the spread of communism. All three forces held great dangers for the immigrant minorities in the region. A handful of men and women were keen to fight for the multicultural ideal and gambled on doing so on the island of Singapore.

There were also others who were prepared to take the same risks, but Lee Kuan Yew was exceptionally equipped to assess the forces of history and harness all that he could in order to establish this new state. He therefore led those who shared his faith, especially those who were committed locals like him. Together, they set out to defend their heritage and use every weapon they could find or forge to do so.

Singapore his only home

Lee Kuan Yew also had an unusual capacity to learn from history. Like many of his generation, he studied the imperial system that the British nation had created out of their commercial and industrial successes in Asia. He understood how their empires claimed universal omniscience while their national interests led them to export their core values. The British sought to transmit those values to the colonials they ruled over, much as the Romans did to the feudal states they left behind when their empire collapsed.

With decolonisation after 1945, they sought to extend their ideals to the new members of the Commonwealth of Nations. Lee Kuan Yew was encouraged by some features in that model to try to adapt them to shape the country that would eventually replace British Malaya.

He failed in Malaysia because his Malay counterparts in the Federation of Malaya wanted their own nation and were willing to accommodate their country's Chinese and other minorities only to a limited degree. Thus he was left with a Singapore that had a population that was 75 per cent Chinese. He and his colleagues realised that they had to recalculate afresh the kind of political structure that such a country could have. For Lee Kuan Yew, his deep sense of Singapore as his only home helped him to contemplate the social and cultural mix that he must bring together in order for this state to survive in an intrinsically hostile neighbourhood.

He was local and his ancestors were embedded in the region. He was educated to adapt to a global maritime empire that had now become Anglo–American. His people were largely Chinese whom he could count on to draw on Chinese traditions if and when forced to stand together in the face of common dangers. He was confident that they were rational. He believed he could educate them to appreciate how enriching a plural society can be.

He thus sought to recapture their aspirations while inducing them to understand the necessity for the republic to be a multiracial and multilingual state. The unique conditions that the country faced called for decisive and innovative leadership that he was determined to provide at all costs.

A new global city–state

Lee Kuan Yew insisted that he was a pragmatist without an ideology. But his understanding of history gave him hope for a new kind of global city–state. Such a city has to be one that consists not only of generations of the local-born who call Singapore home but is also open to the in-migration of peoples who, no matter what their origins, could provide the skills it needs.

The composite state that he has left to his successors would have to be one that is nation in form but not narrowly bound the way the original European model was designed to be. It would have to be one that is better adapted to a resurgent Asia in which new notions of nation, region and transnational enterprise are now possible.

This is an exceptional time when options are still open. Lee Kuan Yew has left behind a vision of the future that is rooted in his past. This is a vision that he would expect his followers to go forward to realise. ℘

Wang Gungwu is University Professor of the National University of Singapore, Chairman of the East Asian Institute, and former member of the Board of Governors of the S. Rajaratnam School of International Studies (RSIS), Nanyang Technological University, Singapore. An earlier version of this article appeared in The Round Table, London (2015).

Reflections on Lee Kuan Yew:
His Legacy on the Public Service

By Eddie Teo

Synopsis

Mr Lee Kuan Yew made the Public Service an efficient and honest institution, globally respected and second to none, which could work with the political leadership to ensure Singapore's survival, sovereignty and independence.

With Mr and Mrs Lee Kuan Yew at the Perth Airport Lounge, 6 April 2007. Photo by courtesy of Eddie Teo.

Commentary

THERE IS much that Singapore and Singaporeans have to thank Mr Lee Kuan Yew for. Today, I wish to thank him for what he has done for the Public Service. He laid the foundation, and built the first few stories of an institution that is now globally respected, second to none, and the envy of many governments. By the time I joined in 1970, Mr Lee already had 11 years to shape the Public Service into one which he thought Singapore should have — an efficient and honest institution which could work closely with the politicians to ensure Singapore's survival, sovereignty and independence.

Right from the start, Mr Lee was very clear that the Public Service should be cleaned up and turned into an incorruptible and meritocratic institution. As former president SR Nathan said, Mr Lee was not so much a visionary, as someone who had the uncanny ability to anticipate, prepare for, and solve problems, for the nation. He lived, thought, felt and breathed for Singapore, 24/7.

For Singapore's survival and progress

He knew that for Singapore's survival and continued progress, public servants had to be recruited and promoted on the basis of ability, not connections. Hence, he retained the Public Service Commission, but replaced promotion on seniority with promotion through merit. He wanted the service to have the best brains and to have a fair share of our top students. Knowing that character was as important as intellectual ability, and being fully aware of human fallibility, he beefed up the Corrupt Practices Investigation

Bureau (CPIB) to ensure that once recruited, public servants remained straight and honest. It was only much later that he added the incentive of high public service salary.

Mr Lee firmly believed that to ensure his Government was incorruptible, anti-corruption laws had to apply to everyone, regardless of rank and position. Having watched how other newly-independent countries went downhill, Mr Lee realised that the best way for our public servants to imbibe the DNA of incorruptibility was for the political leaders themselves to stay clean. The then-Cabinet Secretary once told me that there was a salesman from a company selling executive jets who annually sought to interest Mr Lee in buying a jet for his official use. After several rejections, the salesman gave up. Like many of his older colleagues, Mr Lee lived simply, frugally and unostentatiously. And he never moved out of his Oxley Road home to a bigger mansion.

What working with Mr Lee was like

What was it like to work with Mr Lee? Many senior public servants feared him, and felt intimidated by him, given his piercing eyes, sharp questions and high expectations. When I first took over as Director, Security and Intelligence Division (SID), I was a green 31-year-old, untutored in how to relate to Mr Lee. Thirty-seven years later, I still recall our first telephone conversation. I do not remember the content of that conversation, but it must have been a criticism or query on a paper we had sent out, because Mr Lee made it a point to question every report SID put out for about a month, and less frequently after that. That was his way of testing you. When you passed the test, he eased off a little.

Everyone who worked for him would say how much they learned from him. For me, listening to the discussions he had with foreign visitors I brought to see him was a lesson in geopolitics which no university education or book could match. Many foreign visitors left impressed, awed and mesmerised by the depth, breadth and practical relevance of Mr Lee's analysis and comments. When I accompanied him on his official trips abroad, the way he stood up to other foreign leaders and defended Singapore's interests, made me proud to be Singaporean.

Mr Lee had that balance of a great leader which a Harvard professor taught about — the ability to have a big picture on any issue and yet to zoom in on details when necessary. Other public servants have testified to his deep knowledge of details in areas of their expertise, often surpassing that of the technocrat. In my domain, he appreciated assessed intelligence and was occasionally interested even in operational details.

Another side of Lee Kuan Yew

There was another side of Mr Lee which not many people knew. This was his unwavering support for politicians and public servants who were loyal to him and otherwise doing their job well, but like all human beings, made mistakes. In that sense, he was more caring and less ruthless than people made him out to be. Mr Lee kept people on for a very long time once he felt comfortable with them and deemed them able, trustworthy and loyal. And when they lost an election or retired, he would quietly seek another job for them.

He showed appreciation mostly in his deeds rather than with words. He never praised you directly for a job well done. If you were lucky, you get to hear about how he thought of you through third parties. This would sound strange to our younger officers, who nowadays expect feedback of their performance all the time.

Mr Lee also kept in touch with people whom he considered friends and worth meeting and talking to, regardless of protocol. When I was High Commissioner in Canberra, and Mr and Mrs Lee went on their last official visit, he made every effort to meet, or if they were too old and feeble, to at least talk over the phone, with his very old Aussie friends. I found it very touching that Mr Lee, knowing that it would be his last visit to Australia, made that effort to get in touch with all his old friends. Some public servants may recall a stout and spirited defence which Mr Lee made for the Public Service in 1976 against a PAP Member of Parliament (MP) in Parliament who had complained about discourteous, indifferent and bureaucratic public servants. It bears reading because I drew several lessons from his remarks on how he viewed the Public Service and the role of public servants in the traditional, British-derived system of Cabinet government, where public servants could not defend themselves publicly and required politicians to do so, on their behalf.

First, he believed that there was a clear distinction between the role of the politician and the public servant. The MP was supposed to be good at public relations — how to keep his constituents happy whilst having to say "No" to them. But the public servant was an administrator, not expected to excel in public relations.

Second, even back then, Mr Lee made it very clear that he was less interested in a public servant's academic credentials than his other qualities. To quote him: "Can he get a job done? Can he get a team to work with him? Is he a talker or a thinker, or a talker and a doer? The best, of course, is the man who thinks before he expounds and having expounded, he then acts. It has nothing to do with whether he has got a Ph.D. or a School Certificate or even a Standard VI qualification." His remarks were the precursor of his instruction to the Public Service to adopt the Shell system of assessing officers on the basis of Helicopter Quality, Strength of Analysis, Imagination and Sense of Realism — or HAIR for short.

Not torn between duty and conscience

Mr Lee was able to frame an instruction in such a way that no public servant receiving it would find himself torn between doing his duty and listening to his conscience. When I was in Internal Security Department (ISD), Mr Lee took great pains to explain the security needs of an operation to me in such a persuasive and compelling manner that even if there was a political imperative lurking somewhere, it remained in the background and never emerged.

This is a vital skill of a political leader which allows a public servant to act professionally and fulfill his duty with a clear conscience. During the years I served Mr Lee, he never gave me any reason to feel that I was serving the ruling political party at the expense of the nation. When I obeyed and carried out his instructions, it was clear to me that I was serving the national interest.

This is not to say that Mr Lee would expect anything less than total loyalty from public servants. And public servants gave their best to him because Mr Lee's message of survival and nation-building was so compelling and inspiring for anyone seeking to find meaning and purpose in his career. To Mr Lee, the politician's job was to frame policy, with help from public servants, and then to go out to mobilise public support by convincing the electorate that what the government was doing was right. The job of the public servant was to implement that policy so effectively and efficiently, that the public would be fully convinced that it was the best possible way of doing it.

The clarity of Mr Lee's instructions and the certainty and decisiveness with which he moved once a decision was made, was something public servants greatly appreciated. Public servants dread serving an indecisive minister who waits to see how the wind blows in Cabinet or how the public reacts. This is not to say that Mr Lee was inflexible and did not solicit or listen to advice. But those who sought to advise him had better know when and how to do it.

This does not also mean that Mr Lee never listened to advice or could not brook contrary views. He did not want to be surrounded by a bunch of sycophants and "yes men", comprising an echo chamber. He would not respect you if you had no firm position, because he would conclude that you had no guts, no backbone and no principles. Mr Lee taught us not to trust such a person.

A complex multi-faceted personality

Mr Lee was a complex man, with a multi-faceted personality. My perspective of the man was obtained in the years

I worked closely with him, roughly from 1979 to 1994. After that, we met less frequently, apart from an occasional one-to-one lunch at the Istana. The snippets I have shared today cannot possibly do him justice. No doubt there will be many others who knew him better and have worked with him more closely, who will tell their stories and share their views of our great national leader. Only then can we get a fuller picture of Mr Lee's legacy to Singapore, which is wide-ranging and immense, and extends well beyond his impact on the Public Service and our system of public governance. ∞

Eddie Teo is Chairman of the Board of Governors, S. Rajaratnam School of International Studies (RSIS), Nanyang Technological University, Singapore. He is also Chairman of the Public Service Commission who, as a public servant for 37 years, was Director of the Security and Intelligence Division; Director of the Internal Security Department; Permanent Secretary (Defence); and Permanent Secretary for the Prime Minister's Office. This speech to civil servants on 26 March 2015 was delivered three days after the passing of Mr Lee.

The Three Lee Kuan Yews
I Remember

By Chan Heng Chee

Synopsis

Singapore's first prime minister is hard to sum up. Whilst he was tough and a perfectionist, he was respected as the last of the era of the great post-war leaders. The younger generation of Singaporeans should try to understand his pivotal role in the making of Singapore.

Commentary

OVER THE years, I came to know three Lee Kuan Yews: the tough prime minister, the perfectionist writer, and the elder statesman.

The first time I met Mr Lee was in May 1969. I was a young assistant lecturer newly returned from Cornell. The Prime Minister had come to speak to the staff of the University of Singapore. A week earlier, he had been deeply disturbed by the reactions of students who did not seem to understand the gravity and implications of the May 13 racial riots in Malaysia, judging by their questions and mood at his public lecture. The PM was seized by the potential contagious impact on Singapore, then a fledgling nation.

How could he make them understand the stakes and our vulnerabilities? I stood up to say something in defence of the students. Mr Lee dismissed what I said. I came back with another response. Someone who was present mumbled: "She is very young."

Lee Kuan Yew the perfectionist

Mr Lee was seen as a stern, no-nonsense, authoritarian figure. He was respected and feared. He brooked no opposition. He felt the weight of the immense tasks ahead of him. He probably disagreed with and did not like most, if not all, of my writings as a political scientist for the next two decades.

I saw him again after I returned from my posting as the Permanent Representative to the United Nations. I was invited to the Istana with Tommy Koh and Kishore Mahbubani to lunch with him. It was 1993. We ate simply in a small room. There I met a different Lee Kuan Yew. He was putting forth his views on the world. The Cold War was over, the Soviet Union had collapsed, the United States and Europe were triumphalist. He was thinking through his assessment of the new power configuration and what this meant for Singapore.

In hindsight, he was positioning Singapore in the new world order to ensure maximum prospects for its survival. We were his sounding board. He wanted us to challenge his conclusions. I realised then that he was open to argument, but you had to have strong arguments. He was rigorous and robust in arguing back, like an advocate in court. After several lunches, I learnt gradually that his brusque and strong response was his debating style. If the argument was good, he would accept it.

This was demonstrated again in 1995 when he started writing his memoirs. He sent each draft chapter around to a few people to critique. I was one of them. He would ask what we thought of what he had written, and how he could improve it. Was it tedious? Factual errors, statistics, misremembered dates, he took in at once. He accepted comments telling him it was tedious and he would lose the reader's interest.

There were occasions when one or a couple of us would disagree with his reading of an event or conclusion in his analysis of domestic or international developments. Again if the arguments were good he deleted or amended the paragraphs. But it did not end there. He would revise his chapter and send it back to us to ask again: Is this better? Could he improve it further? Only when we had no further comments did he leave the draft.

I was posted to Washington by mid-1996. I received his faxed chapters in the morning. My comments were sent to him by noon. My astonished secretary would come to my office at 2.30pm to say he had sent back the revised version. It was 2.30am in Singapore. This rhythm of exchange was repeated again and again. He was a perfectionist.

Elder statesman

As ambassador in Washington, I accompanied him and Mrs Lee when he visited the United States as Senior Minister and later, Minister Mentor. Whatever his title,

Americans at the highest levels — presidents, secretaries of state, defence or treasury, elected representatives — made time for him. They wanted to hear his assessments of Asia and the world.

Ex-presidents and prime ministers of other countries do not normally get a White House meeting with American presidents. Mr Lee was the rare exception. The captains of industry and business, the chairmen and CEOs too were eager to get a share of his time and insights.

Mr Lee knew how to put a point across that landed the punch and left a strong impression with his American hosts. He never told anyone what they wanted to hear. He told them what he thought. In these meetings, he infused American officials and industry with confidence and trust in Singapore and Singaporeans. He created our brand name, and investments flowed into our country.

Mr Lee was strong and energetic when he came to the United States in the mid-1990s. His visit was the best thing for an ambassador, for his name opened doors. I noticed then that sometimes when asked a question, he would admit frankly that he did not know the answer. He was a mellower and more philosophical Lee Kuan Yew.

Last of the era of great post-war leaders

I came to know how close and devoted he was to Mrs Lee. He was touchingly solicitous of her and more so as she became frail after her first stroke. But her presence calmed him. Later, after her death, he himself turned frail. In 2010 when he went to Washington to receive the Lincoln Medal, his last trip to the United States as it turned out, he was widely acclaimed as "one of the great statesmen of Asia". Everyone spoke of how he built a remarkable success of Singapore out of so little. The admiration and respect for him and for Singapore were genuine and universal. They saw him as the last of the era of great post-war leaders.

It is hard to sum up Lee Kuan Yew. He was truly a patriot. He worked indefatigably for Singapore. He had the interest of his country at heart. My wish is that younger Singaporeans should read about him, know him and understand his role in the making of our nation. ∞

Chan Heng Chee is a member of the Board of Governors of the S. Rajaratnam School of International Studies (RSIS), Nanyang Technological University, Singapore. She is also Ambassador-at-large and Chairman of the Lee Kuan Yew Centre for Innovative Cities at the Singapore University of Technology and Design (SUTD). She was a political science professor before becoming ambassador to the United States from 1996 to 2012. This appeared in The Straits Times on 25 March 2015.

The Man and His Dream

By Joseph Chinyong Liow

Synopsis

Lee Kuan Yew's indomitable spirit and pragmatism in ensuring Singapore's survival was driven equally by an idealism and vision of an independent island that would be an oasis in an arid Southeast Asia.

Commentary

IN MANY ways, the passing of Lee Kuan Yew brings to a close the formative history of Singapore. Lee, who passed away at age 91, was the island-state's founding prime minister and the last surviving member of a team of indomitable spirits that included Goh Keng Swee, S. Rajaratnam, and Toh Chin Chye. Together, these men, and the people who worked for them, steered newly-independent Singapore through the stormy years of separation from Malaysia in 1965 and the height of the Cold War in Southeast Asia, and in the process, created the vibrant, first world metropolis the world has come to know.

Much has been written about Lee Kuan Yew; the material available on the man and his ideas would easily fill a library. Whether authored by admirers or detractors, the vast majority of what is written about Lee shares one common thematic thread — an emphasis of his hard-nosed pragmatism and instinct for survival. Indeed, Lee's stubbornness and strategic foresight were legendary. Guided by Machiavellian principles, he was never one to cave in to popular opinion, and held the view that leaders should be feared and not necessarily liked or loved.

Paths not chosen

Given this characterisation of Lee — one often repeated by those who worked closely with him — it would seem that trying to detect elements of idealism in his thinking is nothing short of a fool's errand.

The Oxford Dictionary defines idealism as "the practice of forming or pursuing ideals, especially unrealistically". This is not a character trait that one would typically associate with Lee Kuan Yew. I would suggest however, that at an absolutely crucial point in Singapore's history, it was a combination of idealism and vision on the part of Lee and his colleagues that led them to set Singapore on the "unrealistic" path of embracing an independence that was thrust on them, and transforming their island within a generation, from a declining regional entrepôt into a renowned international centre for manufacturing, technology and financial services.

When Singapore was booted out of the Federation of Malaysia on 9 August 1965 and left to fend for itself, what it needed was not a hard-nosed pragmatist, but an idealist with a vision of an independent Singapore that would stand out from its neighbours, all bogged down in the dire conditions that defined Cold War Southeast Asia.

On that fateful day in 1965 — neither the time nor the circumstance of its own choosing — Singapore found itself in an exceedingly hostile strategic environment. A few hours after separation was announced, Malay ultranationalists from Malaysia, keen to take Lee to task for his audacity in questioning Malay supremacy in the country, were already talking about retaking Singapore. Across the Strait of Malacca, Indonesian President Sukarno's Confrontation policy was still in place, aimed not only at Malaysia but Singapore as well. Further north, the Vietnam War was on the verge of escalating.

In essence, as the Cold War was raging, Southeast Asia was bearing the brunt of its "hot" elements, and the Domino Theory articulated a very plausible strategic outcome for the non-communist states in the region, particularly given concerns of Soviet-Chinese collusion (the Sino–Soviet split was not known to the outside world at the time).

Daring to dream

It is easy in hindsight to say that Lee and his compatriots had no choice but to set Singapore on the course of independence. But this claim downplays the seriousness of what confronted Singapore at the time, how carefully alternatives had to be pondered before a path was chosen, and the vision and idealism involved in imagining a course after independence.

Given the strategic circumstances, could the "pragmatist" Lee have chosen to pull his punches during the merger with Malaysia, rather than spend those two years (1963–1965) promoting an alternative social-political-economic order to Malay supremacy, so as to secure Singapore's immediate viability as a political and economic entity as part of Malaysia?

After Separation, could Singapore not have become a satellite of the United States the way South Vietnam was, or a treaty ally like the Philippines? Could it not have chosen the path of "Finlandisation" in order to blunt any potential Malaysian or Indonesian aggression?

All this may seem unrealistic, even ludicrous, in hindsight. But back then, it would not at all have been beyond the pale. In fact, if we consider the policies that smaller states chose during this period — Cambodia, for instance — it could even be argued that any of these postures would be more "realistic" and "pragmatic" than the small island-state of Singapore, without natural resources or a hinterland and vulnerable to ethnic tension, staying independent and on its own. Lee himself said that Singapore was an "improbable, unlikely nation."

Pragmatism to keep the dream alive

But, as we know, Lee Kuan Yew and his colleagues decided to go it alone, against all odds, and Lee's adroit manoeuvering between the United States and the People's Republic of China during those Cold War years eventually ensured that Singapore was able to keep a necessary distance from either camp.

Yet it was Lee's idealistic vision — and those of his colleagues as well — in those early weeks and months of independence that dared to dream a dream that was not dictated by the strategic circumstances. Not only that, it was their idealism that inspired those who chose to remain on the island to believe in the vision that Lee and his colleagues had for a sovereign and successful Singapore.

Doubtless, pragmatism was required in order to keep the dream alive. Lee would go on to develop an international reputation as a politician of singular intellectual ability and fearsome personality, commanding more respect than affection. But back in early August 1965, the dream of a successful, independent Singapore that manages to surmount its innate vulnerability could only have been dreamt by an idealist and a visionary.

And as we remember Lee Kuan Yew's remarkable contributions to Singapore, it would be a great disservice to his memory if we do not consider this aspect of his leadership in those trying, early years. ∽

Joseph Chinyong Liow is Dean of the S. Rajaratnam School of International Studies (RSIS), Nanyang Technological University, Singapore. He is currently also Senior Fellow, Centre for East Asia Policy Studies, and the inaugural holder of the Lee Kuan Yew Chair in Southeast Asia Studies at The Brookings Institution, where this article was first published.

The Sage and Giant from Southeast Asia

By Jusuf Wanandi

Synopsis

The late former prime minister Lee Kuan Yew may not have started warmly with Indonesia and ASEAN, but he eventually became a staunch supporter of Singapore's large neighbour based on the trust developed with Suharto, which anchored the growth of ASEAN. How will the successor generation pursue his legacy?

Commentary

SO MANY things have been said about Lee Kuan Yew. He was the founder of modern Singapore, a small transit harbour on the tip of the Malay Peninsula. Together with his colleagues such as Goh Keng Swee and S. Rajaratnam, he built Singapore from a Third World to a First World country in less than two generations.

Lee was the thinker and strategist of many Southeast Asian policies on the region and the world. On ASEAN, Lee was initially lukewarm, but Singapore now has become one of the many active members, while always leaning on the conservative side.

Lee Kuan Yew's foreign policy

On his foreign policy, he was a true realist, and that is why he wanted to see a balance of power in East Asia, and achieving that purpose meant keeping the US presence in the Western Pacific. In addition, he did his best to assist China in its human resources development by training its bureaucrats and admitting students from China into Singapore's universities. Singapore also invested substantially in China.

Singapore, after all, is a trading nation and so has to keep its relations close to China economically. Lee also watched carefully to keep relations with neighbours amicable, not only through ASEAN but also bilaterally, especially with Indonesia and Malaysia. With Indonesia, Lee managed to build a close relationship with Suharto after a frosty period of seven years, due to his rejection of Suharto's appeal for clemency for two marines who participated in combat during Sukarno's *Konfrontasi*.

Both Lee and Suharto became close as Lee was appreciative of Suharto, who dealt with him and Singapore on an equal basis. On Suharto's part, he thought that Lee would like to help him and Indonesia. He also recognised Lee as a real partner in Southeast Asia, particularly within ASEAN. While Suharto was criticised by the Indonesian elite in the last few years of his rule, it was Lee who defended his friend and appealed to let him stay in power.

Lee's myopic view on the relationship was that it tilted too much to government-to-government relations, especially with the military.

While this might have served Singapore's interest as the role of the government is overpowering, for the Indonesian side that was considered inadequate — especially after Suharto stepped down. That is why Indonesia–Singapore relations remain limited, because Indonesia's public opinion of Singapore is still somewhat negative; so far there have been no substantial efforts on the Singaporean side to deal with and relate to the non-governmental part of Indonesia.

Lee Kuan Yew and Indonesian democracy

Singapore tends to think that it is unnecessary and does not directly serve its interests, but Indonesian democracy is real and the government can do only so much. This can become acute in the future because Singapore's investments in Indonesia have been increasing dramatically, especially in the last decade, and Singapore has become one of the big three investors in Indonesia overall.

Lee, with his sharp thinking, especially on the future of East Asia and Asia Pacific, had become the spokesperson for the region, in particular to the West, and that was indeed an important role that he played. And regarding the future strategic development of the region, no one can replace him.

I am really very fortunate to have known Lee closely during the crisis years after Suharto stepped down. He was always straight-forward in his assessments of Indonesia and Indonesia-Singapore relations, and that was his strength, which added to his credibility in the eyes of others.

People appreciated his thoughts on Indonesia and on its relations with Singapore. Sometimes he could comment on what Indonesians could not even say during the Suharto years about themselves. I learned a lot from him and will always be thankful for my guru's words and advice.

He was the sage and giant not only for Singapore but also for the region. He should be remembered as one of our Southeast Asian leaders that did so much for the region.

Lee's insights and leadership transformed Singapore into a developed nation. Now with a new generation, which has benefited from his creation of Singapore as a city–state, his ideas should be further adjusted, but that is the task of the new leadership he had already prepared for Singapore. Thank you, Mr Lee! ✍

Jusuf Wanandi is a Vice Chairman on the Board of Trustees at the CSIS Foundation in Jakarta, and a founding director of The Jakarta Post where this commentary first appeared.

The Engine That Was Too Big for the Boat

By Kumar Ramakrishna

Synopsis

Former Prime Minister Lee Kuan Yew's renowned intellectual, moral and political strengths played a major role in Singapore's rise from Third World to First in one generation. Fair-minded Singaporeans are unlikely to forget his achievements.

Commentary

NOT LONG after the fall of Soviet Communism more than two decades ago, the American Soviet specialist Jerry Hough created a stir when he declared that "Singapore had actually won the Cold War". In a sense, Hough was paying a compliment to the vision of Lee Kuan Yew, Singapore's first prime minister.

The emerging orthodoxy by the early 1990s was that the US-led Western bloc, organised according to the principles of liberal democracy and market capitalism, had trumped Soviet-style centralised political and economic planning. This was what had won the Cold War, as popularised by Francis Fukuyama's famous "End of History" thesis.

Hough's claim about Singapore was thus startling because while Singapore had adopted market principles in economic organisation, its political system was not liberal democratic in a textbook sense, but rather a hybrid one. Then and now, Singapore's system of governance prioritised order as the basis for the rule of law. Hough was thus implying that there was also a Singapore model of governance that deserved wide appreciation.

Lee's view of order and rule of law

Over the years Lee had had many detractors who chided his failure to adopt textbook liberal democratic methods in governing Singapore. They suggested that by so doing he was undermining the rule of law in Singapore. The critics totally misunderstood Lee's perspective however. Lee saw the rule of law as utterly integral to the successful political and economic development of Singapore. However Lee's view of the rule of law was one that was subordinate to Singapore's needs and not *vice versa*. He rejected an un-contextualized, abstract conception of the law. In particular, the experiences of fighting the Communists in the 1950s and 1960s engendered in Lee the conviction that order must always precede and establish the basis for legal frameworks.

In a speech to the University of Singapore Law Society on 18 January 1962, Lee argued that while in "a settled and established society, law appears to be a precursor of order", in emerging ones wrecked by violence and subversion, the reverse was often the case: "without order, the operation of law is impossible". At the time of this speech, the Cold War was at its height, and Singapore and Malaya were very much a frontline in the ideological and geopolitical conflict between the Eastern and Western blocs.

It was with this wider backdrop in mind that Lee added that the "realities of the sociological and political milieu in Malaya and of the world of 1962 are that if you allow these shibboleths of 'law and order' to be uttered out of context" and without reference to "the actual social and political conditions we are in", disaster may strike, simply because in "the last analysis, if the state disintegrates then the rules of all laws must vanish".

Lee's life mission: Fighting society's entropy

Years later, an insightful journalist suggested that to understand Lee Kuan Yew's approach to governance, one must first appreciate how he had devoted his entire political career to fighting the "entropy" — the decay — of a society and its politics. This was something he had had first-hand experience with during his twilight struggles with the powerful and often violent Communist United Front in the Singapore of the 1950s and early 1960s.

For Lee, the lesson from that struggle — quite clearly the defining experience that shaped his entire outlook on politics and governance — was clear: Singapore needed order as the wellspring of everything else — including especially the economic security that a polyglot, immigrant, multiracial society needed as an initial basis for glueing its disparate elements together.

Lee's ability to instinctively grasp through the "fog" of both the internal political upheaval of the struggle with the Communists, as well as the external instability of *Konfrontasi* of the 1960s — that political order and economic growth were the *sine qua non* of Singapore's survival, was important. It was arguably one aspect of what the renowned

19th century Prussian military philosopher Carl von Clausewitz called *coup d'oeil* — "the rapid discovery of a truth which to the ordinary mind is either not visible at all or only becomes so after long examination and reflection". Lee's uncanny ability to dissect a complex situation under stress and chart a path forward was a measure of his *coup d'oeil*.

But there is another aspect to *coup d'oeil* that is equally important and which Lee possessed in abundance: the "resolution" to overcome "the torments of doubt" and follow through despite the uncertainties expressed by all and sundry. In this respect, many commentators have noted Lee's forcefulness in pursuing courses of action that were often seen as controversial and unpopular. Clear examples are the restrictions on foreign newspapers deemed to have interfered in Singapore's domestic politics; unfettered religious proselytisation; family planning policies that some deemed promoted elitism; and of course, defamation suits against those opponents whom Lee felt had impugned the political credibility he needed to govern optimally.

Singapore's political viability paramount

What arguably tied all these various elements together, regardless of one's sentiments about them, was one overriding consideration: Singapore's continued political viability and prosperity. Lee consistently counseled resolute, eternal vigilance. This was the only stance he believed made sense in light of how the globalised nature of Singapore's economy and polity rendered the country inescapably exposed to global and regional perturbations.

A third element of the *coup d'oeil* that Lee appeared to possess was "presence of mind" — or the innate capacity to surmount the "unexpected" and pursue one's aim to a successful conclusion. Make no mistake: Lee could certainly be pretty Machiavellian in his machinations with his political opponents in pursuit of his agendas. In July 1965, a mere month before separation from Malaysia, *Life* magazine — quoting an unnamed "British high official in Singapore" — somewhat inelegantly described Lee as "the most brilliant man around, albeit just a bit of a thug".

But one must keep things in perspective: in an era when global Communism was elsewhere on the march, the Communists in Singapore — no strangers to cheerfully employing ruses and stratagems themselves to get their way — complained that they had found Lee's PAP a match in "methods of political chicanery". Lee Kuan Yew was no saint and never pretended to be one — but he possessed the "presence of mind" to defeat the Communists and set Singapore on a different trajectory.

As it was said of Abraham Lincoln the day he passed away, Lee Kuan Yew himself now "belongs to the ages". In the 1970s, a leading American politician once declared of Lee and Singapore: "The engine is too big for the boat". Perhaps that may have been the case, but the gratitude of fair-minded Singaporeans is not likely to ever abate. ∞

Kumar Ramakrishna is an Associate Professor and Head of Policy Studies in the Office of the Executive Deputy Chairman, S. Rajaratnam School of International Studies (RSIS), Nanyang Technological University, Singapore.

Chapter II

Lee Kuan Yew
and Foreign Policy

Singapore and Lee Kuan Yew's Worldview

By Ang Cheng Guan

Synopsis

The thinking of Singapore's first prime minister has profoundly shaped the country's foreign policy. It is an embodiment of his worldview.

Commentary

INDEPENDENT SINGAPORE'S foreign policy was shaped principally by founding prime minister Lee Kuan Yew, with foreign minister S. Rajaratnam and Goh Keng Swee, defence and finance minister, when there were economic implications. Indeed historians who have perused the archival documents, both in Singapore and abroad, would attest that it is impossible to reconstruct the history of Singapore's foreign policy without constant reference to Lee because he figures so prominently in most of the documents.

Lee's influence owed to both his strong character and longevity. He died on 23 March 2015 age 91, while Rajaratnam died in 2006 at age 90 and Goh in 2010 also at age 91. Even after he retired as prime minister in 1990, Lee continued to be a guiding force in Singapore's foreign policy through his "mentoring sessions" with cabinet ministers as Senior Minister and later Minister Mentor.

Asia's leading strategic thinker

Singapore's foreign policy can be explained in terms of "agency" — the characteristic mindset of the leader, in this case Lee Kuan Yew, and the intellectual assumptions underlying Singapore's approach to world affairs under his leadership and guidance. This is an explanation of the evolution of Singapore's foreign policy rather than its application.

Lee's tenure as prime minister coincided with the period of the Cold War. His time as senior minister, from 1991 to 2004 and minister mentor from August 2004 to May 2011, fell rather neatly into the post-Cold War period. However Lee had a very well-developed sense of history and a dynamic grasp of geostrategic reality even from the 1950s when he embarked on a political career.

As Lee was so influential in the making of Singapore's foreign policy — the echoes of his thinking can be heard in every single foreign policy speech and interview given by the second and third-generation Singapore leadership — an understanding of his beliefs and premises is imperative for understanding and analysing Singapore's foreign policy.

While much has been written about Lee and his leadership role in the development of Singapore, almost all have focused on his domestic policies and on issues of governance, with very little on his foreign policy thinking.

This is somewhat surprising considering that Lee is generally acknowledged as Asia's leading strategic thinker, one who helps "us find direction in a complicated world".

Pragmatist, not ideologue

Lee had this uncanny ability to foresee the political trends that helped Singapore to be so nimble in the conduct of its foreign relations. On more than on occasion, Lee had said that he was not an ideologue but a pragmatist, and that his thinking and worldview were not shaped by any particular theory but "the result of a gradual growing up from a child to adolescent to a young student to a mature adult".

On the overarching framework which shaped his understanding of international relations, Lee said "It's always been the same from time immemorial". Tribes always fight for supremacy, he explained. Bringing this to its logical conclusion, Lee predicted that by the 22nd century, China and the United States would either have to learn to co-exist or would destroy each other. Although Lee claimed he did not adhere to any theory or philosophy of foreign policy, his overall thinking did resemble that of a "soft realist" — someone who believed in the realist principles about the nature of power but at the same time accommodated perspectives that were liberal or idealist-oriented such as the value of institutions and global cooperation.

Lee's life-long preoccupation was the survival of Singapore. This was his perennial foreign policy challenge — how to "seize opportunities that come with changing circumstances or to get out of harm's way". In his view, to achieve this would require "a prime minister and a foreign minister who are able to discern future trends in the international political, security and economic environment and positions ourselves (Singapore) bilaterally or multilaterally to grasp the opportunities ahead of others".

Lee was prescient in projecting the shifting balance of power from a European Western dominance of the period from the 1500s to the 1900s, to one in which China and India, and Asia in general, would become dominant once again in the 21st century. By 1985, he already foresaw the rise of Asia in the 21st century, anticipated the inexorable rise of China, and to a lesser extent India, with the relative reduction of influence of the Western world.

Survival of the small state

Lee was impressed by the realities of power behind the formalism in the United Nations and other international organisations and the importance of having the ability to enforce sanctions to uphold international law. He saw the need for small states to arrange relationships with bigger countries to ensure their independence and to exercise indirect influence. At the same time, he had a clear vision of the possibilities and limits of multilateral organisations such as the Afro-Asian Solidarity Organisation and Movement of Non-Aligned Nations and the Commonwealth of Nations.

While acknowledging the need for Singapore to join these organisations to gain acceptance, Lee was realistic about their ability to protect and promote the interests of members against the efforts of the superpowers to divide and patronize them. He always stressed the need for Singapore to be nimble and alert, to ensure that in any arrangement or shifts in the balance of power it had the preponderant force on its side. Starting from first principles, he saw the survival of small states like Singapore as being intertwined with the stability and well-being of their regional neighbourhood and the dynamic balance and economic interaction of the global powers.

Finally Lee Kuan Yew had been very committed to the fundamentals of his philosophy of foreign policy. He had also been remarkably consistent in his views about the balance of power, the inter-relationship between economics and politics, and the role of the great powers in the international system. He certainly had the ability to sense change, for example, the need to cultivate the Americans when the British could no longer be counted on, or the rise of China.

But for all the accolades that have been heaped on him, he professed that he did not know when he started his political life in the 1950s that he would be on the winning side of the Cold War, and that Singapore would be what it is today — an implied reminder of the role of contingency in the study of history. ❧

Ang Cheng Guan is Head of Graduate Studies at the S. Rajaratnam School of International Studies (RSIS), Nanyang Technological University, Singapore. An earlier version of this commentary appeared in The Diplomat, an international current affairs magazine for the Asia–Pacific region.

Lee Kuan Yew and Singapore's Foreign Policy: A Productive Iconoclasm

By Alan Chong

Synopsis

Lee Kuan Yew's mark on Singapore's foreign policy is that of applying counterintuitive strategies to improve the island state's international standing. In retrospect, this has ensured Singapore's long term viability as a sovereign nation-state.

Commentary

AS SINGAPORE'S first prime minister and the point man in negotiating decolonisation from Britain in the late 1950s and early 1960s, Lee Kuan Yew carries an aura of being one of the pioneers of the island state's foreign policy. His political personality appears to have been directly mapped onto his steerage of foreign policy: cold unflinching appraisal of one's circumstances, and self-reliance in designing one's survival strategies, but only up to the point that external parties can be persuaded that it is in their conjoined interests to partner Singapore in pursuing win-win collaborations.

Lee's autobiography reveals the profile of an energetic, enterprising young man who was confronted with a series of personal challenges in adapting to material scarcity and political brutality, especially during the Japanese Occupation. This was a key formative influence for foreign policy born of dire geopolitical and geoeconomic circumstances.

Not a normal country

Independent Singapore, bereft of a reliable hinterland constructed by the British empire, was literally perceived by its leaders as an island unto itself, surrounded by similarly decolonised but territorially larger nation-states. The initial decade of transiting from colony to independence from 1959 to 1965 was traumatic on a national level. By his own admission, Lee's initial view that 'island states were political jokes' had to be reversed to achieve the impossible. His strategy for a sound foreign policy was to think unconventionally, and in word, to act as an iconoclast — a leader who sets the pace for his followers with a knack for the counterintuitive.

In his own reflections in 2011, following three decades as Prime Minister, then Senior Minister and Minister Mentor, he emphasised the need for Singaporeans to grasp foreign affairs:

> *I'm concerned that Singaporeans assume that Singapore is a normal country, that we can be compared to Denmark or New Zealand or even Liechtenstein or Luxembourg. We are in a turbulent region. If we do not have a government and a people that differentiate themselves from the rest of the neighbourhood in a positive way and can defend ourselves, Singapore will cease to exist. It's not the view of just my generation but also those who*

have come into Defence, Foreign Affairs Ministries and those who have studied the position.

Already in 1966, he was urging students at the then-University of Singapore to aspire to bigger dreams in their careers. This would add value to Singapore by enticing the world to take interest in its industry, development, standards of living and sometimes, sheer intellectual insights. He went on to argue that once the great powers and Asian states planted intellectual, scientific and commercial stakes in the island state, Singapore's fundamental security would be assured indefinitely.

In this sense, Lee shared with his friend and PAP comrade, S. Rajaratnam, an affinity for global imagination — Singapore could literally treat the world as its hinterland if its people and their technical skills were capable of servicing the world's niche requirements in banking, telecommunications, research and development (R&D) and indeed diplomacy.

Lee the philosopher of foreign policy

As Lee would have it, international affairs were all about leadership and the making of either good or bad decisions. In a less publicised speech at the Australian Institute of International Affairs, he set out the view that:

> *"International Affairs" is as old as the subject of man... [T]he essential quality of man has never altered. You can read the Peloponnesian Wars, you can read the Three Kingdoms of the Chinese classics, and there's nothing new which a human situation can devise. The motivations of human behaviour have always been there. The manifestations of the motivations whether they are greed, envy, ambition, greatness, generosity, charity,*

inevitably end in a conflict of power positions. And how that conflict is resolved depends upon the accident of the individuals in charge of a particular tribe or nation at a given time.'

On hindsight, this was more than a fitting epitaph for the first prime minister of the Republic of Singapore. It was a statement of a belief in the possibilities of forging one's own destiny. We call it today the Singapore Dream of peace and stability, folded into the SG50 milestone of progress and prosperity. Singapore's foreign policy under Lee's astute sense was certainly man-made.

Lee's approach to foreign policy has always been guided by a quixotic mixture of principles of anxiety, nationalistic zeal, and an earnest attempt to dovetail the national interest with some universalist principles circulating in the international order. These compass points have not been clearly prioritised for ostensible reasons of bureaucratic and diplomatic flexibility, and therein lies Lee's talent for discerning the best path forward for Singaporean foreign policy.

Correct outcomes, not political correctness

Although Lee has never publicly referred to his role in forcing a decision on any particular foreign policy issue, he has never shied away from suggesting that his personal diplomatic heft has enabled him to convey national messages directly to his opposite numbers in foreign governments. The tone of his remarks on relations with China, Taiwan, Indonesia, Malaysia, the United States and Vietnam in his memoirs suggests that his presence as the authoritative decision maker mattered to foreign perceptions of who could effectively steer policies for Singapore.

As Singaporeans and the world mourn the passing of a giant of twentieth century Asian politics, we will do well not to forget that Lee Kuan Yew was never one to entertain political correctness. He was more concerned with producing correct outcomes even amidst the vagaries in international politics. Perhaps the final reflection should be reserved for Lee's views on something as controversial as the United States intervention in Iraq early in the 21st century.

Despite American dismay over their post-invasion quagmire in rebuilding Iraq in 2003–2012, Lee encouraged the United States to complete their mission, notwithstanding his government's initial disapproval of George W. Bush's invasion plans, since fundamentalist Islamic terrorists in Southeast Asia and elsewhere would take heart from an outright American withdrawal.

The erstwhile United States Ambassador to Singapore conceded a grudging respect for Lee's sagacity in a confidential cable in 2006 under the subheading 'Welcoming the United States, but not our politics'. This is Lee Kuan Yew, the successful iconoclast. ဢ

Alan Chong is an Associate Professor of International Relations at the S. Rajaratnam School of International Studies (RSIS), Nanyang Technological University, Singapore. He has published a study comparing Lee Kuan Yew and Mahathir Mohamad as exemplars of authoritative decision-makers in foreign policy.

Pursuing Mutual Strategic Interests: Lee Kuan Yew's Role in Singapore–US Relations

By Ong Keng Yong

Synopsis

The close bilateral ties between Singapore and the United States centred on friendship between Mr Lee Kuan Yew and successive American leaders. He established institutions to pursue strategic interests of both countries in a pragmatic partnership.

With Mr Lee Kuan Yew at the Singapore Energy Conference, 4 November 2008. Photo: The Straits Times © Singapore Press Holdings Limited, reprinted with permission.

Commentary

MR LEE Kuan Yew, who died on 23 March 2015 aged 91, has been the most instrumental factor in the development of Singapore's relations with the United States. In fact, bilateral ties were initially very much centred on the friendship between Mr Lee and successive American leaders who deeply respected his strong conviction, clear big-picture vision and extraordinary strategic leadership.

The Vietnam War could be said to have strengthened Mr Lee's cachet and standing with Washington. Mr Lee saw American participation in the Vietnam War as buying time for non-Communist states in Southeast Asia, and played a role in stiffening United States resolve to resist Communism. Singapore's independent and non-aligned foreign policy orientation gave him great credence within the American policy establishment, as a neutral party supporting their military campaign in Vietnam.

A vital interpreter of events in Asia

Mr Lee remained a vital interpreter of events in Asia long after the Vietnam War ended. His standing in American policy circles has been explained by Foreign Minister K Shanmugam, who notes that Mr Lee recognised some fundamental truths about the United States and the world well before other states and leaders. Mr Lee saw that strong United States presence was vital to maintain peace and balance in Asia as the Asian economies developed, and supported it long before it was fashionable to do so. Singapore was often in the minority of voices, sometimes even alone, in speaking up for the United States in the developing world and forums such as the Non-Aligned Movement.

Later, again under Mr Lee's leadership, Singapore stepped up to help the United States maintain its presence in the region even as it drew down its assets elsewhere. In November 1990, in one of his last acts as Prime Minister, Mr Lee signed a Memorandum of Understanding with then-US Vice President Dan Quayle in Tokyo, offering enhanced use of facilities in Singapore to American military aircraft and naval vessels as a contribution to sustaining United States forward military position in Southeast Asia.

Even as he worked with American statesmen at the strategic level and preserved the balance of power in Asia, Mr Lee saw flaws within American society. Although he praised America's strengths, its enterprising spirit and openness to talent, Mr Lee did not shy away from speaking of America's weaknesses such as the widespread availability of guns, and as he puts it, the breakdown of civil society and erosion of the moral underpinnings of American society.

As American leaders valued Mr Lee's views on geopolitics and the world order, and admired his accomplishment, they have not taken to heart his criticism. In some cases, American opinion makers also agreed with Mr Lee's analysis of the problems troubling their country. They knew that Mr Lee believed in the American can-do way and that the United States is the only country with the strength and determination to deal with the challenges faced by the global community. Even as the United States was affected by the recent financial crisis and its supposed decline, Mr Lee repeatedly reminded others not to underestimate American creativity, resilience and innovative spirit. He is confident the US will find its feet again.

Former United States Secretary of State Henry Kissinger writes:

> … *Lee has made himself an indispensable friend of the United States, not primarily by the power he represents, but by the excellence of his thinking. His analysis is of such quality and depth that his counterparts consider meeting with him as a way to educate themselves... Every American president who has dealt with him has benefitted from the fact that on international issues, he has identified the future of his country with the fate of democracies. Furthermore, Lee can tell us about the nature of the world that we face, especially penetrating insights into the thinking of his region. Lee's analyses shed light on the most important challenge that the United States confronts over the long term: how to build a fundamental and organic relationship with Asia, including China. There is nobody who can teach us more about the nature and the scope of this effort than Lee Kuan Yew... Lee is not only one of the seminal leaders of our period, but also a thinker recognised for his singular strategic acumen.*

A pragmatic partnership to pursue strategic interests

Mr Lee's long-term vision and strategic intellect single-handedly contributed to the cementing of the close ties that Singapore now enjoys with the United States. Singapore and United States officials often articulate that Mr Lee has established the institutions and processes for both countries to pursue strategic interests which would normally be impossible between a small island state and the global superpower. American policymakers would always recall how Mr Lee developed the basis of bilateral defence cooperation, especially access arrangements for American forces in Singapore.

They also believed that it was Mr Lee's persuasive influence which laid the ground for the United States to enter into negotiations with the Singapore government on a bilateral free trade agreement. Through Mr Lee's readiness to meet a large number of officials from the American policy establishment, substantial linkages have been built up which are now permanent and regular exchanges between the Singapore and US authorities.

Differences in policy and governance have surfaced from time to time. There will always be different priorities and emphasis in policy implementation but bilateral ties are now locked into a pragmatic partnership going beyond individual personalities. The solid foundation established by Mr Lee had allowed both countries to focus on the strategic issues and the big picture to substantiate the unique relationship. Ultimately, the ability of Singapore to articulate regional concerns and views, particularly on geopolitical and strategic issues, and to foster consensus in various international forums on common challenges facing the world will ensure a continuous dialogue and cooperation between the two countries.

Singapore leaders will continue to have access to the top policy-makers in Washington. Yet, they would need to establish their own level of influence and strategic value to the United States. Countries in Asia have new leaders who can engage the United States directly and in their own ways. This is different from the situation when Mr Lee was in government. The quality of Singapore's strategic assessment of developments in Asia and beyond will determine the level of confidence, trust and value which American policy-makers will accord to Singapore. ഇ

Ong Keng Yong is Executive Deputy Chairman of the S. Rajaratnam School of International Studies (RSIS), Nanyang Technological University, Singapore.

A US Envoy's Impressions of Lee Kuan Yew

By Daniel Chua

Synopsis

Lee Kuan Yew's conversations with US leaders are not as widely known as his speeches. A report by a US ambassador to Singapore on Lee's October 1967 visit to the United States reveals the extent of Lee's successful diplomacy towards the US.

Commentary

PRIME MINISTER Lee Kuan Yew's first official visit to the United States from 16 to 27 October 1967 was a milestone in Singapore–US relations. Through the visit, Lee developed a better understanding of the American leadership and its people, as well as laid the foundation for economic cooperation between the two countries.

While Lee's speeches and public statements have been compiled and published, records of his meetings with foreign leaders are not as well publicised. Excerpts from a report on Lee's October 1967 visit by the first United States Ambassador to Singapore, Francis J. Galbraith, demonstrate Lee Kuan Yew's ability to persuade and hold his own before American leaders and academics, who were universally impressed by the Singapore leader.

A generous welcome

In his welcome address, United States President Lyndon Johnson remarked that "America welcomes a patriot, a brilliant leader, and a statesman of the New Asia", to which Lee responded: "I am almost embarrassed by the lavish words of praise that you have showered upon my colleagues and me in our modest efforts to build a more just and more equal society in a very difficult corner in Southeast Asia."

On this cordial note, Lee led his delegation to discuss ways that the United States could work with Singapore, especially after Britain's announcement of a military withdrawal from Singapore and Malaysia in July 1967.

In discussions with the president and officials from the Defence and State Departments, Lee was able to convince the United States government to explore possibilities of using former British naval bases for commercial ship repair and maintenance. Both Lee and his American interlocutors agreed that keeping the British in Singapore would be desirable.

But if the British were to withdraw eventually, American use of aircraft and ship repair facilities in Singapore should continue. An American military presence, albeit for commercial reasons, would contribute to a sense of stability in Singapore because of inherent US interests in Singapore's security.

Interacting with American scholars and leaders

Galbraith went on to describe Lee's interaction with audiences at Harvard University, Massachusetts Institute of Technology (MIT) and Columbia University. Lee was "always speaking without notes" and was "well received". According to Galbraith, who was with Lee for the visits:

> Lee's intellectual dimension began to unfold in their company and his exchange with them was obviously something he enjoyed and profited from.

But more than engaging in intellectual discussions, Lee managed to extract a promise from MIT's Jerome Wiesner to send a team of social scientists and technologists to Singapore to explore the development of a Southeast Asian centre for technological education.

Through Lee's speeches and conversations, Galbraith detected a growing empathy towards President Johnson and his Cabinet. "As the visit progressed," reported Galbraith, "his expressions of respect for the President, for Secretary Rusk, for Secretary McNamara, and, though less explicitly, others grew and was less hedged." It was only two years earlier, on 30 August 1965, that Lee had famously rebuked the US administration for its incompetence in resolving the conflicts in Indochina.

During his visit in October 1967, however, Lee was able to appreciate the political culture in America, as well as the domestic pressures that President Johnson faced. Lee absorbed as many lessons as he could through the conversations he had with government officials, academics and students.

Promoting Singapore as an investment hub

Perhaps Lee Kuan Yew's most impressive performance came during a luncheon with businessmen in Chicago, when he made a "pitch for American investment in Singapore". Lee described Singapore as "a good base camp where businessmen could 'leave their expensive machines' and their families in confidence while they sallied forth into the less certain areas".

Galbraith also reported that Lee "amused" his audience with statements such as "you can get a telephone connection with anyplace in the world in five minutes and if you can't, let me know and I'll chop someone's head off!" Lee's message to American businessmen was clear — he wanted to create an image of a "no-nonsense" Singapore government and "a people willing and able to work".

Lee did not wait for US investors to serendipitously discover Singapore as a perfect destination for capital. He seized every opportunity to promote Singapore and stressed the efficiency and quality of the labour force in the country. With his deft diplomacy, Lee Kuan Yew was able to convince American oil companies like Mobil Oil and Esso to build oil refineries in Singapore worth up to US$105 million.

The confidence that American investors had in the Singapore leadership and its people brought in large amounts of foreign investments that pulled Singapore out of the economic debacle created by high unemployment, rapid population growth, loss of jobs due to the British military withdrawal and loss of markets due to Singapore's separation from Malaysia.

First steps towards US–Singapore accord

The October 1967 trip was after all Lee Kuan Yew's first official visit to the United States. Hence, there were aspects of Lee's thinking that the US ambassador felt difficult to accept. "Brilliant as he is," remarked Galbraith, "Lee has some rather blind prejudices and narrow interpretations of history, and his attention is often very hard to command to try to rebut these. But when one can get him to listen, he listens intently and absorbs what one tells him."

Ambassador Galbraith concluded his report with a strong recommendation for the United States government to engage closely with Lee and Singapore. He ended his 16-page report with these words:

"I think it is very important that we find ways to continue dialogue and contact between Lee and our top men in Government and some of our more responsible academic leaders. Through such continued exchange, we may be able to help Lee exert his considerable talents as a 'political educationalist' on other young Asian leaders and potential leaders in Southeast Asia in a way that will enhance their admiration for and exertion of rationality, the most needed commodity of all in the area."

US Secretary of State William Rogers, who served during President Richard Nixon's first term, once said that "Lee Kuan Yew is Singapore". Singapore's national interests were always high on his priorities whenever he engaged with foreign leaders. Lee's dexterous diplomacy not only made Singapore relevant to American interests during the height of the Cold War, but his political acumen provided the leadership for regional security and economic development. &)

Daniel Chua is a Research Fellow at the Institute of Defence and Strategic Studies, S. Rajaratnam School of International Studies (RSIS), Nanyang Technological University, Singapore.

Lee Kuan Yew's China Wisdom

By Hoo Tiang Boon

Synopsis

As the rare statesman who has engaged all five generations of Chinese leadership, Lee Kuan Yew had a deep and profound understanding of China. Policymakers and scholars would do no worse than to overlook Lee's insights on the rising power.

Commentary

AMONG THE many abilities that made Mr Lee Kuan Yew, Singapore's first prime minister, such a valued and influential interlocutor to foreign leaders and governments was undoubtedly his prodigious and masterly understanding of China. Lee was, in the words of Graham Allison, 'the world's premier China watcher'. This is an accolade attributed to the fact that his assessments of Beijing — frank, unvarnished and sometimes contrarian — often proved to be uncannily correct or prescient.

This was a profound wisdom borne out not just from a scholastic and historical appreciation of the nuances and contradictions of China. It was one honed by Lee's more than 30 visits to China, starting from 1976, and unique friendship and access to several of the top echelons of the

Chinese leadership, both past and present. Lee remains the rare statesman who has met with all five Chinese leaders, from Mao Zedong to current President Xi Jinping. Everyone of them since Deng Xiaoping, including Xi, have described Lee as a 'mentor'.

On China's rise

It was thus this blend of ground knowledge, elite relations, historical awareness and intellectualism that enabled Lee to '[spot] the rise of China before anyone else'. Lee believed that once China reversed course to more effectively harness the productive capacities of its people, its rise was only a matter of time.

He had met and found 'very capable minds' during his early visits to China, and could see that once ideology was no longer an encumbrance, China would soar. That was in the 1970s, a time when most people were hardly bullish about China's prospects.

Lee was clear about the psychological underpinnings that fuelled China's rise. At the heart of the Chinese strategic mindset, he noted, was the fundamental belief that China should be the world's greatest power, like how it was before its ill-fated century of humiliation and reigned supreme as Asia's dominant power. Ergo, Lee saw no reason why China would not want, if it could, to replace the United States as Asia's 'number one' power.

But to achieve this goal, Lee did not think China would be 'foolish' and compete with others, in particular the United States, in armaments. Rather, China's strategy would be to 'out-sell and out-build' the rest. Moreover, Lee knew that the Chinese leaders took a long-term perspective on strategic issues, and were prepared to 'bide [their] time' until China becomes powerful enough to 'redefine' the extant order.

One thing Lee did not count on China doing to succeed in its goal is to adopt Western-style liberal democracy. In fact, he was reasonably sure that China would not go down that route, and that 'if it did, it would collapse'. This conclusion stemmed from Lee's recognition that Chinese leaders fear the instability and 'loss of [central] control' which liberal democracy might engender.

Lee himself was not convinced that China should be judged or adopt Western political standards, which he thought do not sufficiently take into account China's past. As he wryly observed, throughout 5000 years of its history, China's rulers 'chopped heads, not count heads'.

It was this sort of thinking which led Lee to conclude quickly that in the wake of the 1989 Tiananmen incident, Deng Xiaoping would act decisively to quell the protests, and that Western diplomatic isolation would not succeed in pressurising China to change its political course.

Leader reader

Lee's reading of the Tiananmen situation was aided by a keen ability to 'figure out' the personalities, thinking and leadership styles of Chinese leaders he met. In Deng, Lee saw a strong-willed leader who was not afraid to make tough decisions when problems came up during China's reform and opening-up process. Five-footer Deng in fact stood so high in Lee's estimation that he considered the former to be 'the most impressive leader he ever met'.

Interestingly, Lee had singled out current Chinese leader Xi Jinping for particular praise. Calling Xi a man with 'iron in his soul' and 'gravitas', Lee saw Xi as being comparable to a leader like Nelson Mandela. Lee's assessment of Xi is telling because in the two years since ascending to the top position in China, Xi has emerged to be widely considered as the most powerful Chinese leader since Deng.

Lee has been described as being 'obsessed' about China. But it is worth emphasising that this was an obsession informed and shaped by a bigger obsession on Singapore's long-term national interests. From the time in the late 1970s when he accurately saw and foretold China's rise, Lee knew that Singapore could not afford to miss the Chinese growth train that was about to take off. As one interviewer of Lee noted, the former prime minister had been 'worried about Singapore being left behind when China got back up to speed'.

It had thus been clear to Lee early on, that with China's impending rise, it would be advantageous for Singapore to get to 'know' the country and its leaders better. This does not mean of course, short of a utilitarian purpose, China held little personal interest to Lee. As a country, China had always occupied Lee's attentions while its size meant that it was simply too big to ignore. But having gazed into and understood the future, China's importance became even more evident to Lee and Singapore.

All this has meant the bequeathment of a legacy and wealth of knowledge on China, captured in Lee's several speeches and interviews as well as writings based on these material. While China is an evolving creature, future generations of China watchers as well as policymakers would do no worse than to overlook Mr Lee Kuan Yew's insights. 🕉

Hoo Tiang Boon is an Assistant Professor with the China Programme, and Coordinator of the MSc (Asian Studies) Programme at the S. Rajaratnam School of International Studies (RSIS), Nanyang Technological University, Singapore.

Lee Kuan Yew and India's Turn to Pragmatism

By C. Raja Mohan

Synopsis

Although it had long disappointed Lee Kuan Yew, India's contemporary rise in Asia and the world has much to do with the adoption of economic and strategic pragmatism that the founder of modern Singapore never tired of recommending for Delhi.

Commentary

DELHI WAS irritated if not angered when Lee Kuan Yew held up a harsh mirror to India's self-defeating economic and foreign policies in the 1970s and 1980s. Personally close to the Nehru–Gandhi dynasty, Lee privately advised them to be more pragmatic and publicly criticised India's failures. Lee's trenchant critique, however, was rooted in a genuine affection for India, clear recognition of its potential to shape the economic and political order in Asia and the world, and deep frustration at Delhi's seeming inability to act in self-interest.

India's economic slumber, its perpetual domestic chaos, and the temptation of its political elites to blame democracy for all its ills had some influence on Lee, who held 'democracy and development' were incompatible at least in the early stages of nation-building. As India evolved in the later decades, Lee's impatience yielded to better appreciation of its complex internal dynamics and the role of democracy in managing them.

Lee sceptical but supportive

Delhi's reluctance to lend military assistance to Singapore when it became independent, disappointed Lee. If he saw India as the successor to the British Raj in providing security to smaller states of Asia, he was deeply surprised by Delhi's lack of a strategic ambition and its inability to engage in regional realpolitik. Lee was also critical of India's policy of non-alignment and its steady drift towards the Soviet Union from the 1970s. He was deeply concerned about the impact of India's closeness to Moscow on Southeast Asia's security environment in the 1980s.

When India embarked on the path of economic liberalisation and globalisation at the turn of the 1990s, Lee was sceptical but supportive. Lee was not confident that India can easily shed the burdensome legacy of state socialism accumulated since independence and quickly construct a liberal economic order at home. Lee met all the Indian leaders in the reform era from Narasimha Rao to Narendra Modi, frequently visited India and continually encouraged them to press ahead with reforms. Despite many setbacks to Singapore's own commercial engagement with India, Lee never gave up hopes for India's economic transformation.

In the early 1990s, India also sought to catch up with the economic dynamism in Southeast Asia that it once looked down upon. Rather than turn its back on India, Singapore became one of the strongest advocates of India's integration with Asia. P.V. Narasimha Rao articulated the "Look East" Policy in his Singapore Lecture (1994) that Lee presided over. More than a decade later, Prime Minister Manmohan Singh publicly thanked Singapore for holding India's hand at a difficult moment and facilitating its integration with all the ASEAN-led institutions, including the ASEAN Regional Forum and the East Asia Summit.

Lee's vision of India's role

As India began to generate higher economic growth rates in the 1990s, Lee was increasingly confident that India's rise was inevitable. He also saw it playing a crucial role in stabilising Asian balance of power amidst the rise of China and the strategic vacillations of America. In 2007, Lee noted that India was not seen as a threatening power in Southeast Asia, essentially because of the nature of its political system, thereby tempering some of his earlier critique of the Indian democracy.

Lee's greatest contribution was probably to make Singapore loom very large on India's economic and foreign policy radar since the 1990s. His calls on Delhi over the decades to lift the heavy hand of bureaucracy, avoid economic populism, and claim a leadership role in Asia were long rejected by the Indian political elites.

Today, those ideas of Lee are very central to Indian discourse. While few in the Indian intellectual or policy elite agree with Lee's critique of democracy, his emphasis on good governance, eliminating the scourge of corruption, sustaining communal harmony are widely accepted today as critical for the nation's progress towards peace and prosperity.

Lee's stress on pragmatism and his deep suspicion of ideologies, of all kinds, now resonate with an ever larger numbers of the Indian political elite. Many state chief ministers like Chandrababu Naidu of Andhra Pradesh, Manohar Parrikar of Goa, and Narendra Modi, current Indian Prime Minister, have absorbed the ideas of Lee in developing their own approaches to governance. It is a pity Lee will not be around to see how Prime Minister Modi, who perhaps comes closest to his notions of pragmatism, might take India forward.

Adopting Lee's strategic pragmatism

As he opened up Singapore to India's talented professionals and growing middle classes, the city–state has acquired an extraordinary salience in India's world view that is way above its size and weight. In the process, Lee has helped India rediscover its historical connections to Asia and renew its acquaintance with greater China. If modern Singapore was seen by the British Raj two centuries ago as a vital link in the trade between India and China and between the Indian and Pacific Oceans, Lee actively egged on Delhi to cultivate a practical relationship with Beijing and end the prolonged stagnation in bilateral relations.

If Lee and Singapore want India to be more engaged in Asia, Modi has renamed India's 'Look East' Policy as 'Act East Policy'. This is not merely a change in nomenclature, but the reflection of a new commitment to contribute to the maintenance of Asian security order. Unlike his predecessors, Modi is eager to strengthen the security partnerships with the United States and its allies in Asia, develop middle power coalitions, and lend support to weaker states. At the same time, Lee would also be pleased with Modi's decision to discard many of India's past inhibitions on economic cooperation with China.

If India in the past, had no time for Lee's suggestion that Delhi must claim the mantle of the Raj in securing Asia, Delhi now declares itself as a 'net security provider' in the Indian Ocean and the Asia Pacific. Although India would never move at a pace that Lee would have liked, it has begun to advance thanks to its adoption of strategic pragmatism that the founder of modern Singapore never stopped recommending for India. ∞

C. Raja Mohan is a Distinguished Fellow at the Observer Research Foundation, New Delhi, and heads its Strategic Studies Programme. He is an Adjunct Professor at the S. Rajaratnam School of International Studies (RSIS), Nanyang Technological University, Singapore, and a visiting research professor at the Institute of South Asian Studies (ISAS), National University of Singapore.

Lee Kuan Yew's Leadership: Model for China?

By Benjamin Ho

Synopsis

Singapore's governance model is widely touted to be world-class. Much of it is due to the brand of its political leadership which is studied by many countries around the world, not least China.

Commentary

DESPITE BEING the last country in Southeast Asia to formally recognise the People's Republic of China in 1990, Sino-Singapore relations are highly advanced; the city-state engages deeply with China in multiple dimensions of bilateral ties — economic, cultural and political. Both countries' heads-of-state are also scheduled to visit each other this year to commemorate 25 years of bilateral relationship.

The relationship was built up in large measure by the first prime minister Lee Kuan Yew, beginning with his path-breaking visit to China in 1976 when he called on Chairman Mao Tse-tung. In his condolences to the Singapore government over the passing of Mr Lee Kuan Yew, Chinese president Xi Jinping described Lee as an "old friend to the Chinese people [who is] widely respected by the international community as a strategist and a statesman" as well as the "founder, pioneer and promoter of China–Singapore relations".

Lee Kuan Yew's leadership as a model for China?

Notwithstanding his opposition to the Communist Party of Malaya in the 1950s and 60s, during the early years of the People's Republic of China, his friendship and goodwill with subsequent Chinese leaders grew, most notably Deng Xiaoping, whom he first met in Singapore in November 1978. Lee described Deng as the "most impressive leader I have met". In his memoirs, Lee recollected that he had "never met a communist leader who was prepared to depart from his brief when confronted with reality... At 74, when he was faced with an unpleasant truth, [Deng] was prepared to change his mind." This included changing China's view of Singapore, which till then, was perceived as a "running dog" of the West.

As noted by Harvard's Ezra Vogel: "A few weeks after Deng visited Singapore, this description of Singapore disappeared... Instead, Singapore was described as a place worth studying for its initiatives in environmental preservation, public housing, and tourism." And Lee went on to persuade Deng to call off the CCP's support for the CPM's insurgency in Malaysia, Thailand and Singapore.

Indeed, China's benevolence towards Singapore over the past two decades should not be explained as simply for securing markets for its economic exports or for geo-strategic reasons. The focus, instead was on domestic governance insofar as Singapore represented a model of efficient and effective government that provided prosperity and stability for its people. In 2012, President Xi ordered China Central Television to produce a series on Singapore for the benefit of Chinese learning.

Studies in Chinese leadership patterns have shown that a paternalistic leadership model to be most reflective of indigenous Chinese preferences. Defined as a type of leadership that combines strong and clear authority with concern, consideration, and elements of moral suasion, such a leadership style is identified with transformational leadership, one that places the leader as the agent of transformation, whereas the organisation and the followers are the target of the transformation.

Transformational leadership also obliges the leader to transcend the individual interests of the followers, while at the same time uniting them behind the collective interests of the organisation, a posture that befits the Confucian ideal of the sagely king or the superior gentleman. The Chinese saying, "If a leader sets a bad example, subordinates are likely to follow suit" (*shangliangbuzheng xialiangwai*) relates well to both Singapore and China, societies that are — in varying degrees — influenced by Confucian thought patterns.

Indeed, the need of a strong — and upright — leader features prominently in Chinese politics, more so when at stake is the effective governance, survivability and prosperity of a country of 1.3 billion people. Not merely as servants of the state reflecting and representing the will of the people, the Chinese leader is expected to lead the nation, to the extent of over-riding popular will, if he deems necessary.

Lee Kuan Yew as leader par excellence

Lee's decision-making process can be best summed up on the basis of "what works" — often defined by stability and orderly progress — rather than "what is demanded" by popular opinion. Lee's disdain for the "marketplace of ideas" was also seen in the manner in which he selected his inner circle of political confidantes regarding policy-making matters. Lee's "three orbits of leadership" as observed, comprised of an inner ring whose members were Goh Keng Swee, S. Rajaratnam, and Toh Chin Chye; the second and third orbits consisted of allies he respected and trusted and those who have proven themselves competent.

In Cabinet meetings, he valued quality of opinions more than the quantity of votes, as Lee himself puts it, "In the Cabinet, I would say there were about five or six strong ministers with strong views. And you want to get a consensus if you can. If you can't, then you get the majority in numbers: I would prefer the strong ministers to back the policy. If one or two strong ministers strongly felt, very fervently, against the policy, I would postpone it because I would take their objectives very seriously".

Strong leadership, in Lee's mind, also meant not bending to the pressures and interests of external powers, particularly that of more powerful countries. This was crucial in the early years of Singapore's independence in which it had yet to establish deep ties with the international community.

Former head of the Singapore public service, Lim Siong Guan, who served under Lee, relates how Lee had instructed him in the conduct of the country's foreign affairs:

> Lee told me that in the course of my work, I would be dealing with foreigners, and advised: 'Always look the foreigner in his eyes. Never look down. You are dealing with him as a representative of Singapore. Conduct yourself as his equal.'

Leadership transition in both Singapore and China

Given Lee's towering influence on Singapore's political scene, Singapore's political transition from first to third generation of leaders has been remarkably smooth — an attribute that is also shared by the ascension of President Xi Jinping to power, notwithstanding the factional differences that are the hallmark of one-party systems. This is where comparisons between Singapore and China end.

Given the changing social demographics in Singapore and the opening up of its socio-political space, the one-party model that has served Singapore for the past 50 years since its independence cannot be indefinitely taken for granted, as various scholars have observed.

But for China to acquiesce to such proposals for liberal political reforms is unimaginable, given the present climate where President Xi is said to wield unprecedented power, both personal and within the party. As Elizabeth Economy puts it in a recent *Foreign Affairs* article, if Xi's reforms could yield a "corruption-free, politically cohesive, and economically powerful one-party state with global reach", it would be like "a Singapore on steroids". Whether China is able to achieve the Chinese Dream remains to be seen, but what is certain is that the political legacy bequeathed by Lee is instructive for China's future. **ॐ**

Benjamin Ho is an Associate Research Fellow in the Multilateralism and Regionalism Programme, S. Rajaratnam School of International Studies (RSIS), Nanyang Technological University, Singapore.

A Towering Inspiration for China

By Zha Daojiong

Synopsis

Lee Kuan Yew has been a towering inspiration for China's modernisation. His emphasis on stability in governance resonated well in China.

Commentary

A LEGENDARY tale has it that Deng Xiaoping was so astonished by the changes he witnessed on his visit to Singapore in November 1978 that he made up his mind about opening and reforming China by learning from Singapore. In his youth, Deng had once made a stopover in Singapore on his sea journey to France. The visual contrast could not have been stronger.

Lee Kuan Yew was the founding father who made possible his country's transformation. Two years earlier, in 1976, Lee had travelled to China, in spite of the absence of formal diplomatic ties between the two countries. In his lifetime, Lee made 33 trips to China, each personalising his own commitment to make a positive contribution to China's pursuit of modernisation.

Source of inspiration

Lee Kuan Yew built a country — small in geographical size and with virtually no natural resources beyond sustaining basic human survival — into one to be respected not only throughout Southeast Asia but also worldwide. If anything, the country Lee Kuan Yew led, governed and then advised even after retirement from the prime ministership, has proved its resilience throughout the decades of profound challenges in its neighbourhood and beyond.

Singapore's record of rising from the ashes serves as a source of inspiration, partly owing to the fact that ethnic Chinese are the majority in the Singaporean society, many of whom — Lee's own family included — had migrated to that part of the Malay Peninsula when China was the 'sick man of Asia': as a people, the Chinese can prevail out of adverse circumstances, just like other peoples of the world. It is up to the Chinese in China to prove that they too can match their achievements with those of their Singaporean cousins by kinship and cultural ties.

Today, the catch phrase for that inspiration is 'soft power'. Singapore is, beyond dispute, one of the tiny number of countries that truly attracted China, its government and populace. It was only natural for the Chinese government to choose Singapore to be one of the first destinations for Chinese citizens to go on private foreign travel in the early 1990s. Singapore was not just a place with Chinese-speaking communities, but visibly a successful country. The more the average Chinese could learn from Singapore, the better they could contribute to improving China.

Teacher of governance

Lee Kuan Yew gave priority to maintenance of social and political stability in governing his country. Among other points of wisdom in him as a national leader, the necessity of stability in governance resonated more closely in China.

As a matter of fact, compatibility in governance approaches led China to seek Singapore's assistance in training Chinese civil servants. Such training programmes cover wide-ranging topics, from economic policy to project management, from community management to fighting corruption; virtually every aspect of governance was covered in these programmes. Transfer of ideational/technical expertise from Singapore to China has become systematic.

For China, learning from Singapore comes with a unique cultural environment. Under Lee Kuan Yew's leadership and personal example, civil servants of Singapore dealing with China are required to be fluent in Chinese as one of the four official languages which include English, Malay and Tamil, while Malay is the national language. This facility in Chinese greatly helped the participants from China in their interactions outside the formal classroom, an attribute unavailable in many other advanced economies.

In the wider world, the match in governance between Singapore and China has received mixed commentaries, including some critical ones. But Lee Kuan Yew and his successors stood their ground and, arguably, have prevailed.

China is solely responsible for shortcomings still existent in its own society. The appeal of building a clean government, with Mr Lee as a leader and his country as a model, continues to be strong.

Singapore in China

In April 1994, Lee Kuan Yew, as Senior Minister, inaugurated the China–Suzhou Industrial Park, in China's Jiangsu province. For China, this 'Singapore in China' project was conceived as a tangible demonstration of modernisation. Chinese planners envisioned 2012 to be the year for the collaborative Suzhou project to reach comparable Human Development Index levels of Singapore in 2011.

The initial years of the Suzhou project did not live up to Singaporean expectations. It was the fundamentals in bilateral relationship Lee Kuan Yew had built up that helped it to continue. The emphasis on pragmatism, another hallmark of Lee Kuan Yew's leadership, helped to navigate both sides of the partnership.

Today, 'Singapore in China' projects have spread to other cities including Tianjin, Guangzhou, and Shenyang. In numerous other Chinese industrial zones and beyond, the Singaporean presence is strong. The value of these projects goes beyond statistical records of trade and investment. Throughout the times of uncertainty that the outside world had perceived China as a global economic partner, Lee Kuan Yew and his government cast a vote of confidence.

The one thing Lee Kuan Yew had for sure shown China and the Chinese society is that countries do not have to be large and strong in the conventional sense of the term to be valuable. Mr Lee is going to be remembered as a towering source of inspiration. ๛

Zha Daojiong is a Professor of International Political Economy, School of International Studies, Peking University. He was a Visiting Senior Fellow in 2009 and 2011 at the S. Rajaratnam School of International Studies (RSIS), Nanyang Technological University, Singapore.

Lee Kuan Yew and Suharto: How Mutual Trust Fostered Bilateral Ties

By Barry Desker

Synopsis

The excellent relations between Indonesia and Singapore from the 1970s were fostered by the mutual trust that developed between President Suharto and Prime Minister Lee Kuan Yew.

Barry Desker (second from left) welcoming Mr Lee Kuan Yew at the Singapore Global Dialogue organised by RSIS, 22 September 2011. Photo by RSIS.

Commentary

OVER A period of almost thirty years from the 1970s, an excellent bilateral relationship existed between Indonesia and Singapore. While it is unfashionable among historians to credit 'great men' for the outcome of events and to look instead into factors underpinning broad historical trends, the smooth bilateral relationship owed much to the mutual confidence which developed between President Suharto of Indonesia and Prime Minister Lee Kuan Yew.

Before that, relations between the two countries had been rocky under Indonesia's first president Sukarno. Prime Minister Lee Kuan Yew's first exposure to Indonesia occurred in August 1960 when he made an official visit to Indonesia and was a guest of President Sukarno. It was a disappointing exchange as Sukarno did most of the talking and there was little substantive discussion, with Sukarno expounding his concept of 'guided democracy', repeating points he had made in many public speeches. The visit highlighted the decline in the Indonesian economy following the expulsion of the Dutch community in 1957, the nationalisation of foreign enterprises and the proclamation of a policy of economic nationalism.

Period of confrontation and turmoil

Indonesia's policy of *Konfrontasi* — Confrontation — after the formation of Malaysia in 1963, resulted in a sharp decline in Singapore/Indonesia trade, arising from Indonesia's ban on trade with Malaysia. Singapore's dependence on its entrepôt role resulted in a sharp economic downturn, even though the impact was limited by continuing barter trade with the Riau islands. There were also more than fifty bomb attacks in Singapore by Indonesian infiltrators.

Turmoil in Indonesia followed the failed coup attempt on 1 October 1965 by the Indonesian Communist Party and its allies within the Indonesia military. This resulted in a counter-coup led by General Suharto. However, General Suharto did not immediately takeover and only formally became President in March 1968.

These negative experiences shaped Mr Lee Kuan Yew's initial perceptions of Indonesia, which loomed large as a threat to post-1965 independent Singapore's existence. Such perceptions were reinforced when sections of the Indonesian military urged a seaborne invasion of Singapore in October 1968 if Singapore went ahead with the execution of two captured Indonesian marines Osman Mohamed Ali and Harun Said, responsible for the MacDonald House bombings, and whose court appeals against the death penalty had failed.

Cooler heads prevailed in Indonesia. Strong diplomatic and personal appeals were made but Singapore proceeded with the executions, which led to mass demonstrations in Jakarta and the sacking of the Singapore embassy.

Improved bilateral ties

Bilateral relations improved significantly when Prime Minister Lee Kuan Yew made his first official visit to Indonesia in May 1973. His 'four eyes' private meeting convinced Mr Lee that Mr Suharto was determined to focus on Indonesian economic recovery. While Mr Suharto demonstrated a willingness to treat Singapore cordially, Mr Lee highlighted the need for mutual trust.

Mr Suharto observed that Indonesia had no territorial claims on Singapore and Mr Lee won his confidence by pointing out that Singapore did not see itself as a Third China (after the People's Republic of China and Taiwan) and emphasised Singapore's rightful role as a Southeast Asian state.

Mr Lee Kuan Yew grew more positive of Mr Suharto over the years. In his dealings with Singapore, Mr Suharto enjoyed credibility because he upheld agreements that he made. The first experience of this was when Mr Suharto sent a message in his early years of office seeking 10, 000 tonnes of rice to meet emergency needs because of the failure of the rice crop. He promised to repay in kind in due course.

Although the price of rice rose on international markets, Indonesia repaid the rice on schedule and provided rice of better quality than that which was given. Singapore's leaders concluded that Mr Suharto was a man who could be trusted. It was an experience repeated at various times during his tenure of office.

In 1978, when there was an attempt to bypass Singapore on the kangaroo route between the United Kingdom and Australia under Australia's newly proclaimed integrated civil aviation policy, which cut access to Singapore while providing inducements to Indonesia and other countries in the region, Mr Suharto took the firm view that ASEAN should not succumb to such tactics.

Similarly, in 1990, when Singapore offered the use of facilities in Singapore to American military aircraft and naval vessels as a contribution to the continued United States presence in Southeast Asia following the return of Clark airfield and Subic naval base to the Philippines, Mr Suharto's public acceptance of this move quelled criticism from the region.

Lee's respect for Suharto

While Mr Suharto did not throw his weight around, he was the most influential leader within ASEAN. Mr Lee respected Suharto because he was consistent and provided space for each ASEAN state to develop in its own way. In this, Mr Suharto practised the Javanese dictum, *mikul dhuwur, mendhem jero* (to look for the best in others and to forgive the trespasses of those whom we respect).

On several occasions, Mr Lee mentioned that Mr Suharto had never reneged on a commitment, even if it was politically difficult. It meant that Mr Lee was aware of the limits of Indonesia's willingness to agree to proposals from Singapore. President Suharto's objections led to the derailing of proposals for an ASEAN free trade area at the first ASEAN Summit in 1976, but his support facilitated the declaration at the fourth ASEAN Summit held in Singapore in 1992 that an ASEAN Free Trade Area (AFTA) would be established within fifteen years.

On Mr Suharto's part, he regarded Mr Lee as a friend, who spoke clearly, could be relied upon and whose judgement was valued. Because of Mr Suharto's support and direction to his officials, negotiations for joint projects such as the Batam Industrial Park, Bintan Beach International

Resort, the Riau Water Agreement and the Air Combat Manoeuvring Range in Pekanbaru proceeded smoothly.

When Mr Suharto visited Batam and Bintan Beach, he observed that the swift implementation of factory and hotel development proposals by foreign investors demonstrated Singapore's honesty and reliability. Mr Suharto saw Mr Lee as a man of his word, who could be trusted to uphold his commitments.

Differences in trying times

But differences did occur. Following the Indonesian invasion and occupation of East Timor in December 1975, Singapore was the only ASEAN country to abstain while the remainder joined Indonesia in opposing a UN General Assembly resolution deploring Indonesian military intervention in East Timor. This created some strains in the bilateral relationship.

In the aftermath of the Vietnamese invasion and occupation of Cambodia in December 1978, Indonesia consistently took a softer position than the other ASEAN countries partly because Indonesia saw Vietnam as having a shared revolutionary heritage gaining independence through the force of arms rather than through consultations with the colonial regime and partly because President Suharto was suspicious of Chinese support for the Khmer Rouge and regarded Vietnam as a bulwark against China. However, Mr Suharto's strong support for ASEAN resulted in Indonesia consistently backing ASEAN positions, surprising critics of ASEAN who felt that a common ASEAN position was not sustainable.

The most trying period in the relationship between Mr Lee and Mr Suharto occurred during the Asian Financial Crisis in 1997–98. When the Thai meltdown occurred in July 1997, the financial panic spread across the region. Although he had stepped down as prime minister, Mr Lee tried to counsel Mr Suharto's children, who took gross advantage of their father's position for economic benefits and were the subject of criticism by the International Monetary Fund (IMF), the American government and international fund managers.

Mr Lee noted that Mr Suharto did not see his children's actions as a problem because he saw himself as the sultan whose children were entitled to these privileges. Nor did Mr Suharto heed the advice of Mr Lee and other leaders not to appoint B.J. Habibie as Vice-President in 1998, as Habibie's penchant for costly high-tech projects worried the financial community.

Lee seen as true friend

Following the riots in Jakarta in May 1998, President Suharto stepped down. Significantly, a few days before his decision, Mr Suharto described himself as being prepared to step down using the Javanese term *lengser keprabon* (to abdicate, usually following dynastic struggles in Javanese courts), highlighting the Javanese mind-set which under-pinned the way President Suharto framed his dealings with the world — an aspect that Mr Lee made an effort to understand.

Mr Lee kept up his relationship with Mr Suharto until Mr Suharto's death in 2008. He credited the strong economic growth in Southeast Asia from the 1970s to 1990s to Mr Suharto's policies and his focus on stability and the economy as well as building excellent relations with his neighbours. In retirement, Mr Suharto regarded Mr Lee as a true friend, one held in high respect by him and his family. ෨

Barry Desker is Distinguished Fellow, S. Rajaratnam School of International Studies (RSIS), Nanyang Technological University, Singapore. He was Dean of RSIS and Director of its predecessor Institute of Defence and Strategic Studies from 2000 to 2014. He was Singapore's ambassador to Indonesia from 1986 to 1993. A version of this appeared in The Straits Times on 8 April 2015.

Lee Kuan Yew's Legacy: His Impact on Singapore–Malaysia Relations

By David Han

Synopsis

The late Mr Lee Kuan Yew's legacy on Singapore–Malaysia relations will continue to have an impact on the diplomatic ties of these two countries. In particular, his insights on the shared geography, history, culture, and the regional and geopolitical contexts for both Singapore and Malaysia will endure for many years to come.

Commentary

THE PASSING of Singapore's founding prime minister Lee Kuan Yew marks the end of an era in the relations between Singapore and Malaysia. But his legacy will continue to shape the republic's foreign policy towards its immediate neighbour, and his views will still be an important lens through which to understand their bilateral ties.

For Mr Lee, the shared realities of geography, history, culture, and the wider regional and geopolitical contexts would continue to underpin Singapore's relations with

Malaysia. Indeed, at the core of his view on Singapore's policy towards Malaysia is the over-riding concern of the republic's continued survival as a nation; the preservation of its territorial integrity; and economic prosperity, *vis-à-vis* its larger northern neighbour.

Fundamentals of Singapore–Malaysia relations

The story of Lee Kuan Yew's political career is almost synonymous and inextricably tied with the history of Singapore–Malaysia relations. Right from the start, when he became the first prime minister of Singapore in 1959, he was already aware that Malaya — as Malaysia was then known — was a crucial hinterland for the economic survival of Singapore. By virtue of geographical proximity and shared colonial history, the economic, social and cultural dynamics of both countries were deeply intertwined. Mr Lee understood that for Singapore to survive economically, Singapore must merge with Malaya, which it did when Malaysia was formed in 1963.

However, the merger was short-lived and ended when Singapore separated from Malaysia on 9 August 1965. The key reason for the split was that Mr Lee's vision for a "Malaysian Malaysia", which championed multiracialism, was incompatible with the race-based policies and communal politics in Malaysia which favoured the bumiputras.

For the past 50 years, though the issue of race and ethnicity has surfaced on a few occasions, it has not severely damaged Singapore–Malaysia ties. Overall, both Singapore and Malaysia have exercised much restraint and sensitivity towards one another on the subject of race and ethnicity.

After separation, Singapore successfully overcame its economic woes and transformed itself into the prosperous city-state it is today. Although Malaysia did not remain the hinterland for Singapore due to the separation, Mr Lee's insight on the close economic interdependence of the two immediate neighbours is still valid. Singapore's largest trading partner is Malaysia and good economic cooperation is vital to both countries. The ongoing Iskandar development project is a testament to the strong economic links of both countries. Singapore and Malaysia also cooperate widely in other areas such as tourism, education, environmental issues, culture, and so on.

Managing bilateral issues

To be sure, there have been contentious disputes over the past five decades. These include the problem of water supply; the withdrawal of contributions of Malaysian workers from the Central Provident Fund (CPF); ownership of Malayan Railway (KTM) Land and Customs, Immigration and Quarantine (CIQ) issues; bridge replacement for the Causeway; and the question of sovereignty over Pedra Branca. Nevertheless, Mr Lee's pragmatism, which is also shared by Malaysia, has been the key to overcoming the periodic tensions which arose in the past and may likely continue in the future.

The current excellent relations between Singapore and Malaysia under the leadership of Prime Ministers Lee Hsien Loong and Najib Razak is a clear indicator that cordial relations based on rationality and pragmatic interest will prevail over emotional and irrational attachment to narrow ethnic or communal agendas in the future.

As both Singapore and Malaysia are close neighbours, regional dynamics have been crucial factors for the foreign policies of both nations. For Mr Lee, a peaceful and stable Southeast Asia, characterised by cordial economic and diplomatic cooperation among Southeast Asian states without interfering in each other's internal affairs, was vital for Singapore's sovereignty and survival. Accordingly, Mr Lee contributed significantly to the development of ASEAN so that ASEAN countries can work together towards regional goals in the ASEAN Way.

Singapore, Malaysia in the ASEAN context

Similarly, Malaysia has always recognised the importance of ASEAN for regional stability which would be conducive for advancing the national interests of Malaysia. It is also in the context of ASEAN that both Malaysia and Singapore can seek to improve their bilateral ties. Such similarities in viewpoint should continue to form a common ground for cooperation between Singapore and Malaysia, and for furthering the interests of ASEAN as a whole.

On broader geopolitical issues, Mr Lee saw that while competition between the United States and China is inevitable, conflict is not. He held the view that the United States should help China to transit into the international community in the spirit of cooperation.

Indeed, peaceful and good ties between China and the United States without major conflicts would benefit Singapore's economic development and survival. Singapore has strong economic ties with China, while it also maintains close military and economic relations with the United States. Singapore's cooperative and hedging behaviour is motivated by its desire for both China and the United States to maintain peaceful ties, and not for Singapore to be forced to choose sides.

Likewise, Malaysia also shares broadly similar strategic concerns with Singapore. Malaysia too has strong economic relations with China, and close military ties with the United States. Good China–US ties would serve the interests of Malaysia as well. Given these overlaps, Singapore and Malaysia can work together, within the context of ASEAN, to engage both Beijing and Washington to enhance mutual understanding and peaceful cooperation in the Southeast Asian region.

Continued relevance of Lee's views on bilateral ties

Lee Kuan Yew's views of relations between Singapore and Malaysia would continue to be relevant though not the key factor that shapes relations between Singapore and Malaysia.

The leadership of both countries should be mindful that the shared geography, history, culture, and regional and geopolitical contexts would always be crucial components that shape Singapore–Malaysian relations. A pragmatic and realistic outlook should consistently undergird and drive peaceful and constructive relations of the two countries, and not allow issues coloured by historical baggage or narrow domestic interests to hinder the relations of the two close neighbours. ✌

David Han is a Research Analyst with the Malaysia Programme at the S. Rajaratnam School of International Studies (RSIS), Nanyang Technological University, Singapore.

Lee Kuan Yew's Economic Legacy: Lessons for Aspiring Countries

By Pradumna B. Rana & Chia-yi Lee

Synopsis

A key legacy of Lee Kuan Yew has been to enshrine good governance (effective government) as an important ingredient of economic development and prosperity. Aspiring countries will, however, face challenges in adopting the Singapore development model.

Commentary

DEVELOPING COUNTRIES have much to learn from Lee Kuan Yew, the first prime minister of Singapore who transformed the republic from a third world economy to one of the most advanced countries in one generation. The lessons for countries aspiring to learn from the Singapore development model are clear — strengthen institutions and improve governance. But this is much easier said than done. To begin with, aspiring countries need to improve the rule of law so that no one is above the law of the land. Equally crucial, they need to reduce corruption as corruption is regressive — small and medium-sized firms pay higher amounts in bribes than large firms.

Thirdly, they need to reform public institutions such as the civil service, bureaucracy, and public administration. Fourthly, they also need to improve the environment affecting the private sector through regulatory reforms, reforms of labour markets, and provision of clearly-defined property rights. The dilemma is that such reforms generate benefits only in the longer term, making them hard for policymakers and politicians with a shorter time horizon to set as priorities. Yet, without them, other policy measures to support sustained economic growth will become less effective and ultimately unravel.

Importance of good governance

The Singapore model of good governance is well-recognised. Development theorists of the past were of the view that economic development could be explained solely by factors like the availability of natural resources, high levels of saving and investment, and openness to foreign trade and investment.

More recently, the Growth Report, published in 2008 by the Commission on Growth and Development headed by Nobel laureate Michael Spence, has found that an additional factor has also to be good governance, based on mainly Singapore's development experience under Lee. As Senior Minister Goh Chok Tong, who participated in the Commission, puts it, for a delicious dish "besides having the right ingredients and the right recipe, you must have a master chef".

Economic development does not just happen. It must be consciously chosen as an overarching goal by the government. Good governance means a government that delivers political and economic stability, implements the correct macroeconomic policies, articulates a vision for the country and implements it. This requires a capable, committed, and credible government, governments that people can trust in, and leaders who are above the board. An abundance of natural resources is neither necessary nor sufficient for a country's economic development. What is required is good governance.

A case of good governance is Lee's choice of the Singapore development model in the 1960s and beyond.

The Singapore development model

After the separation from Malaysia in 1965, Singapore was similar to a typical Third World country of today. GNP per capita was about US$300, unemployment rates were high, and racial disharmony was rife. The announcement by the British in 1968 that they would withdraw their forces from Singapore was also expected to aggravate the unemployment situation further. How should jobs be created?

As the prime minister of a small country, Lee was always thinking big and making bold decisions in the interest of the country. Lee adopted a development model based on export of labour-intensive manufactured goods to world markets. Lee invited multinational companies from all over the world to invest heavily in Singapore. Produce in Singapore and sell to the world, he told them.

To provide an attractive investment environment, the government built the appropriate infrastructure, cut tariffs and quotas, offered tax incentives, and implemented appropriate macroeconomic policies. The Economic Development Board was established in 1961 to provide a business-friendly environment to foreign investors and to convince them that Singapore was a good place to invest. The National Wage Council was also established in 1970 to make sure that the benefits of foreign investment were shared and also to accelerate Singapore's move up the development ladder. Mr Lee also met foreign investors regularly and listened to them and their grievances.

Although pragmatic, Lee's choice of an export-oriented development model driven mainly by foreign investment was a risky strategy at the time. This is because in the 1960s and 1970s, foreign investment was not welcome in the developing world. The dependency theorists, in particular, argued that foreign investors from developed countries typically exploit cheap labour and extract natural resources of the developing countries. It is only after the success of the Singapore development model that export-oriented development strategies driven by foreign investment has been popularly adopted all over the world.

'It's not how you start but how you arrive'

In the 1980s and the 1990s, the type of investment Singapore sought to attract shifted gradually from labour-intensive industries (e.g., garments, textiles, and wigs) towards more high-tech and knowledge-based industries (e.g., chips, wafer fabs, and disk drives). Lee noted that, since the unemployment problem had been overcome, the new challenge was "how to improve the quality of the new investments and with it the education and skill levels of our workers".

Lee's attempt to make Singapore the Asian financial centre and global business hub is also bold. Unable to compete with Hong Kong then, Lee tried especially hard to convince foreign bankers and international financial institutions to come to Singapore by establishing integrity, efficiency, the rule of law, reliability, and stability. In his words:

> *"[The] history of our financial centre is the story of how we built up credibility as a place of integrity, and developed the officers with the knowledge and skills to regulate and supervise the banks, security houses and other financial institutions...."*

Overall, Lee's development strategy which focused on strengthening institutions and improving governance was successful. Other developing countries will, however, face difficulties in adopting this strategy. A case in point is South Asia. Countries in this region had begun their reform programmes in the early 1990s by focusing on macroeconomic areas — monetary and fiscal reforms, and industrial deregulation — which had contributed to a more rapid economic growth. These reforms, however, eventually ran out of steam — because of red tape, endemic corruption, and the lack of rule of law — and have contributed to the recent economic slowdown. Lee's model followed his dictum, which he shared with the King of Bhutan:

> *"It's not how your start the journey that counts, but how you arrive."*

Pradumna B. Rana is an Associate Professor and Coordinator of the International Political Economy Programme, and Chia-yi Lee is an Assistant Professor at the S. Rajaratnam School of International Studies (RSIS), Nanyang Technological University, Singapore.

Right Lessons, Wrong Lessons: Africa and Lee Kuan Yew's Legacy

By Greg Mills

Synopsis

Singapore's transformation from Third World to First stands out as a model to African countries. Still there is a danger that African leaders take the wrong lessons from Singapore's success.

Commentary

"ONE OF the asymmetries of history," wrote Henry Kissinger of Lee Kuan Yew, "is the lack of correspondence between the abilities of some leaders and the power of their countries." Kissinger's one-time boss, Richard Nixon, was even more flattering. He speculated that, had Lee lived in another time and another place, he might have "attained the world stature of a Churchill, a Disraeli, or a Gladstone".

In other words; it was a shame Lee had a small country. Yet it is precisely because Lee did run a small state that Singapore's transformation from third world to first, to use the title of his autobiography, should stand out as a model to African countries of transformation, against the odds and their colonial inheritance.

Singapore's lessons for Africa

Still there is a danger that Africans, especially their leaders, take the wrong lessons from Singapore's success. In 2008, when living and working in Rwanda for President Paul Kagame, I was asked to prepare a summary of Singapore's key lessons. The island-state it seemed, despite the obvious differences to landlocked Rwanda, was an attractive development analogue.

Like its Southeast Asian counterpart, Rwanda is small, densely populated and largely without resources. Both have had to confront crisis. While Lee had steered Singapore from the political turmoil of the failure of the Malaysian Federation in 1965, Kagame's Rwanda Patriotic Front had taken over amidst extraordinary crisis in 1994, a genocide, a terrible failure in controlling ethnic and racial diversity, a feature which Singapore has also had to manage.

A combination of the orderly discipline of Singaporeans, their leadership and bureaucracy with a catalytic role for the state in business, such as through the US$180 billion Singapore investment company Temasek, potentially offered another more interventionist development route to that preferred by Western donors. Singapore's mandatory Central Provident Fund savings scheme promoted by Lee, which enabled the building of public housing on a grand scale, also seemingly offered a way around the chronically low savings' rate in Rwanda as elsewhere in Africa.

Kagame seemed among those leaders who, admirably from this author's vantage, like Lee, were concerned with the finest detail of government, leaving nothing to chance. Certainly, there is much to learn from Singapore's rapid transition from a malaria-ridden swamp to an innovation and technology leader. By 1970, in just five years from independence, Singapore's per capita GDP had increased to $950, and unemployment was under three per cent. By the turn of the century, per capita GDP was $24,000; in the five decades since independence, per capita GDP has increased not less than thirteen-fold in real terms.

Danger of wrong lessons

There is, regardless, a danger that Africans routinely take the wrong lessons from Lee and from Singapore. The first of such 'wrong lessons' is that an authoritarian government is necessary for growth or for difficult decisions to be made. Yes, the island like others in the region — including South Korea, China, Indonesia and Taiwan — has modernised under a system of rigid political control. Still, Singapore has enjoyed extraordinary freedom of individual choice and economic openness, a gentle autocracy quite distinct from usually violent and corrupt African eras of authoritarian rule of which Lee himself was critical.

Moreover, while some might like Lee's 'big man' image, the reality of Singapore is far more nuanced in involving much more than one person and fundamentally being reliant on institutions in the pursuit of development. Although Lee presented the articulate public face and adroitly managed the politics and personalities, his was a formidable team.

Lee's memoirs are testament to how highly he regarded the opinion of his colleagues and how often there were differences of outlook within government on key issues.

Additionally, Singapore made sure that the best and brightest were attracted, that they were paid properly, and they were given full support by leadership to do their job. As Lee observed 'equal opportunities for all and meritocracy, with the best man or woman for the job, especially in leaders in government', were 'basic principles that have helped us progress'. With delegated power and authority went responsibility of course.

In contrast to the xenophobia and identity politics suffered in Africa, the importation of talent has been another key aspect. From a little over one million people at independence, of Singapore's current population of 5.3 million, around 1.5 million are expatriates, permanent residents or migrant workers. The injection of immigrants is part of a strategy to maintain GDP targets, and synchs with need for Singapore's continuous innovation and efficiency.

Singapore's right lessons

Singapore is a 'right lesson' also in the continuous search for competitive advantage. A very flexible labour market helps companies to withstand external shocks, changes and challenges, driven by a philosophy that 'it is better to have a low-paying job than no job at all' — a political anathema in contemporary South Africa, to take one African example. In Singapore, too, a symbiotic relationship is structured between government, the unions and business.

All this has been underpinned by a drive to globalise rather than nationalise. Whereas African countries routinely make it difficult to move goods in and out and are inherently suspicious of the motives of foreign investors, Singapore has capitalised on its strategic geographic crossroads by matching policies and the focus of institutions: There is zero tariff on imported goods; low tax rates; a range of free trade agreements; vigorous trade and export promotion; and nearly 40,000 international corporations on the island, including 7,000 multinationals.

Singapore has avoided trying to buck the markets or the needs and sensitivities of multinational companies and international finance. To the contrary, it has always acted to strengthen regulatory institutions to negate any perception of developing country risk.

African governments like to cite Singapore as an example in the maintenance of their own parastatals and 'partystatals' (companies owned and/or run by ruling parties), both routinely notorious in crowding out private sector competition to the advantage of narrow financial and patronage interests. Again, such lessons are wide of the mark. Even though it is government-owned for example, Temasek's strategy and role is based on commercial rather than political rationale.

Forward looking legacy

Singapore is thus a 'right lesson' for Africa in leadership, planning, continuous innovation, commercial logic and using its only natural resource — its people and minds — to best effect.

By the 1990s, Singapore's per capita GDP was higher than that of its erstwhile colonial master Britain. Today Singapore has the world's busiest port and is the third-largest oil refinery. Under Lee's leadership it has shown what is achievable with better choices in little more than a generation.

A remarkable aspect in Singapore's transition is in its unwillingness to look back. Whereas many African nations berate colonialism at every turn (not least since it offers the prospect of aid and of externalising their problems and excusing regime inadequacies), Singaporeans seldom mention history as an excuse.

Perhaps Lee's greatest legacy was to set Singapore in a direction looking forward. In so doing, he has left an extraordinary legacy, for his own country of course, but also for others aspiring to follow a similar development path. ଛ

Greg Mills heads the Johannesburg-based Brenthurst Foundation and is most recently the author of Why States Recover *(Pan Macmillan, 2014). In 2014, he was a Senior Visiting Fellow at the S. Rajaratnam School of International Studies (RSIS), Nanyang Technological University, Singapore.*

Chapter III

Lee Kuan Yew and Nation-Building: What Next?

Politician, Lawyer:
Will the Legal Culture Endure Him?

By Kevin YL Tan

Synopsis

The significance of law embodied the politics of Lee Kuan Yew. Trained as a lawyer, Lee's politics, in fact, was not based on law, but founded on it. He did not believe that laws had inherent autonomous values, but saw them as tools that could be used to secure the state. In so doing, he created a legal culture in which the public has come to expect government to act in accordance with law.

Commentary

LEE KUAN Yew was a politician first, and a lawyer second. This was so even though he started his professional life as a lawyer before he became a politician. Lee's legacy extends into constitutional law — a subject where the interplay between law and politics is most pronounced. Constitutional theorists have long argued that constitutions are made in heightened moments of political consciousness, mass mobilisation and idealism, and embody the spirit of the nation writ large. Lee never saw it that way.

For him, law was not an autonomous subject with inherent normative content. Neither was it an unqualified good in itself. For him, law was useless unless it served the society in which it operated. His attitude was shaped by his brand of pragmatic utilitarianism, sharpened by his own personal experiences. In that sense, he took an instrumentalist approach to law.

Lee Kuan Yew, the lawyer

Lee's mother told him that he should study to be a professional, so that he would not end up like his father, having to work for someone else. He tried his hands in economics — first at Raffles College, and then at the London School of Economics. But he did not enjoy life in hectic London, and after a year, moved to Cambridge where he read law with great success.

There he preferred the practical subjects, like contract and property law, over more abstruse subjects like Roman Law or the English Legal System. He had little patience for legal theory. Lee did well, scoring a double-first with a Star for Distinction in Part II of the Cambridge Tripos. He was called to the Bar at the Middle Temple in 1950 and returned to Singapore where he commenced practice in the firm of Laycock & Ong in 1951. Four years later, he founded the firm of Lee & Lee with his wife, Kwa Geok Choo and his brother, Lee Kim Yew.

Lee specialised in contract, criminal law and arbitration but did not really enjoy his time as a practitioner, feeling that he was 'selling' his skills 'for a living' and considering it 'an unfulfilling profession'. But it was as a lawyer that

Lee launched his career as a politician. He volunteered his services to the many disgruntled trade and students unions, made a name for himself in the Fajar trial and very quickly became their preferred lawyer and confidante.

Law as legitimating tool

Lee knew that legality — especially if backed by popular will — was a powerful legitimising force. Deployed skillfully, law could be used to legitimise his regime and actions. Take for example, the matter of the 1962 Referendum. There was nothing in Singapore's 1958 Constitution requiring that a referendum be called to determine any matter whatsoever. But when his People's Action Party (PAP) split in 1961, and when the Barisan Sosialis leaders took the matter of Singapore's impending merger with the Federation of Malaya to the Decolonisation Committee and the United Nations, Lee decided to act.

Against objections from within his own party, Lee decided to push ahead with the Referendum Bill in January 1962, taking the chance that it would be defeated. The Bill went to Select Committee and was debated on for nine long days — often with sessions stretching to midnight — before it was eventually passed on 12 July 1962. And when the Barisan accused the PAP of not respecting the people's free will since they had no option to reject merger, Lee argued, with cool lawyerly logic:

> In the course of the last 17 years since 1945, no one has ever suggested that Singapore should be independent by itself. It is a political, economic and geographical absurdity ... It was the perfidy of the British in their desire to hold on to a military base

at the tip of the Malayan Peninsula, which would give them command of the whole area, that decided them on this cruel political amputation, one which the logic of geography, economics and military necessity compels them now to withdraw from.... Since nobody denies that we must be together, then I say that there is no denial of an expression of free will in asking the people to choose the form of the merger they like.

The Referendum was a resounding success for the PAP, and despite the continuous protests from the Opposition, the legitimacy of the merger was secured. No one challenged the legality of the referendum.

Lee understood the Rule of Law to embody the first two of three principles laid down by the great Victorian jurist, Albert Venn Dicey: (a) that no person can be punished except according to the law; and (b) that no person is above the law. The third Dicyean proposition — that the common law was the source of the constitution — was not relevant, since Singapore had a written constitution, unlike Great Britain. Beyond these assertions, law could, and should, be moulded according to the demands and peculiarities of each society. In this way, law was used to legitimise political action.

State formation and survival

The modern creation of states is founded on law. Politics provided the impetus for their formation, but the actual constitution of the state is more often than not law. Singapore's independence from Britain was effected by the British Parliament passing the Malaysia Act 1963, and the corresponding agreement by the Federation of Malaya, Singapore, Sabah and Sarawak entering into the Malaysia Agreement.

And when Singapore was negotiating its separation from the Malaysian Federation, a legal agreement would ultimately determine the terms of the Separation. For this important task, Lee despatched two of his most trusted and able lieutenants — Goh Keng Swee and EW Barker. Barker had, prior to entering politics, been a partner in Lee & Lee and he was entrusted with making sure that the Independence of Singapore Agreement (more commonly referred to as the Separation Agreement) would be drafted fairly.

Barker, who had known Lee since their days together at Raffles Institution, remembered how, when Lee asked him to join Goh Keng Swee in negotiating the Independence of Singapore Agreement, Lee constantly reminded Barker to make sure that he 'locked in' the 1961 and 1962 water agreements between the Public Utilities Board of Singapore and the State of Johore, and have the Agreement sent quickly to the United Nations Secretariat and lodged with the Treaties Registry. Barker did this, working it into clause 14 of the draft Constitution and Malaysia (Singapore) Amendment Act, 1965 which the Malaysian Parliament passed on 9 August 1965.

Land acquisition

A major plank in the People's Action Party's (PAP's) 1959 election platform was a programme of industrialisation and mass building of public housing. This required the Government to compulsorily acquire large tracts of land, clear the squatters and make them available for industries and housing. While Singapore was part of Malaysia, this proved impossible because Article 13 of the Federal

Constitution gave all Malaysians a right to property. Thus, the owner of any property acquired by the Government must be compensated at market rates, making the whole programme expensive, even untenable.

So, when Singapore seceded from the Federation in 1965, Lee ensured that Article 13 would not become part of Singapore law. When Parliament passed the Republic of Singapore Independence Act in December 1965, importing all the fundamental liberties provisions in the Federal Constitution into Singapore, the right to property was intentionally omitted. This enabled the Government to pass the Land Acquisition Act in 1966, and proceed speedily with its industrialization and housing programmes.

Law and institutional design

Despite his British legal training, Lee was neither a traditionalist nor a sentimentalist. The British parliamentary system worked in Britain but was, as far as he was concerned, unsuitable for Singapore. For a start, the rule that a Member of Parliament could resign from his party, cross the floor and still remain in Parliament, almost proved to be Lee's undoing. After the PAP split in 1961, the PAP's majority was reduced from 43 out of 51 to a mere 30. Further defections and the death of PAP Minister Ahmad Ibrahim brought the PAP's number of seats down to just 25. This cut too close to the bone and Lee moved to amend the Constitution to ensure that any MP who resigns or is expelled from his or her party, loses his or her seat as well.

Lee worried incessantly about the need to protect the minorities from discrimination, and to this end, created the Presidential Council of Minority Rights, and then later, instituted the Group Representation Constituency (GRC) system. The first was inspired by an earlier Kenyan example, while the second was a new innovation that sought to marry majoritarianism (i.e., no reserved seats for minorities) and minority representation.

And when he witnessed a 12 per cent vote swing against the PAP, he worried that an unworthy non-PAP party would come to power, promote cronyism and engage in pork barrel politics, and squander Singapore's reserves. Lee looked to the law again, and used the Constitution and created a new political creature called the Elected President, with veto rights over spending and appointment of key appointment holders.

The jury system

Lee was not a fan of the adversarial system of justice, especially the jury system. In such a system, he was convinced that it mattered not whether his client was in fact guilty, but that he succeeded in persuading the jury that he was not. The jury trial had been part of Singapore's legal system since 1826, and had its roots in a time when judges travelled on circuit and were not familiar with the place or people where a trial was being held. A group of locals would be summoned to sit as a jury to determine the truth of what was being said in court. The jurors became the determiners of fact, while the judge determined the law.

Lee knew that juries were easily impressed and persuaded by skilful and eloquent lawyers like David Marshall and himself. Winning a case was all about being able to sway the jury. It had nothing to do with whether a defendant was right or wrong. After one successful case, Lee felt disgusted with himself for enabling his client — whom he was sure was guilty — go free. He vowed to get rid of the jury, which he did in 1969.

Legal culture to endure beyond him

This short reflection is not a study of Lee's entire legal legacy. That would require an entire tome unto itself for his role in shaping Singapore's legal landscape has been enormous. Lee was an excellent and practical lawyer, and while he eschewed a profession in the law for a life in politics, his lawyerly instincts never left him. He knew that law gave legitimacy to political action and provided a stabilising force to the vicissitudes of political life.

Lee and his colleagues created Singapore out of a political struggle, and then proceeded to build it on the basis of law. Today, Lee's fingerprints are everywhere in the legal system, but by founding a nation on law, he and his colleagues have created a legal culture that will endure beyond him. Politics must be conducted on the basis of law, not because of any pre-ordained rules, but because the public has now come to expect it. 🙨

Kevin YL Tan is an Adjunct Professor at the S. Rajaratnam School of International Studies (RSIS), Nanyang Technological University, Singapore, and at the Faculty of Law, National University of Singapore. He is the editor and author of over 30 books on the law, history and politics of Singapore.

Singaporean Singapore: What Next after Lee Kuan Yew?

By Bilveer Singh

Synopsis

While the physical transformation of Singapore from Third World to First is well-known, Lee Kuan Yew's lasting achievement was building a Singaporean nation out of its diverse people. What next post-LKY?

Commentary

WHEN MR LEE Kuan Yew visited the Central Sikh Temple on 2 November 1990, I was just a few feet away as the then-Prime Minister remarked: "At the right time, my Government wants the Sikhs to have the Punjabi Language (as a Mother Tongue Language in schools). My Government and I would be failures if we foist the Chinese language on you." That was Lee Kuan Yew the nation builder.

True to his words, one of his last acts as Prime Minister was a letter to the Sikh community indicating the Ministry of Education's willingness to accept Punjabi as a Mother

Tongue Language as part of the national bilingualism policy in the context of multiculturalism. Throughout his entire political career, Lee Kuan Yew had also scrupulously kept true to this policy as he strove to build a nation out of a multi-ethnic society.

Unity in diversity

Lee Kuan Yew never feared confronting realities. One of the eternal hard truths of Singapore was its sharp fault lines along racial, religious and linguistic lines. To him it was clear that without developing a sense of unity among the populace, the island Republic would fail to take off politically and economically. Worse still, it faced the danger of imploding from within as experienced by similar plural societies such as Sri Lanka, Lebanon, Cyprus and Fiji.

Lee Kuan Yew never forgot the ethnic origins of Singaporeans either. He deplored the colonial policy of ethnic enclaves. British colonial policy towards a plural society was to allow people to mix and not integrate. People came together but remained separate, holding on to their respective religions, cultures, languages and orientations.

Even as an Opposition leader in the 1950s, Lee Kuan Yew realised the danger of this policy. On becoming Prime Minister in 1959 he reversed it, creating the nation-in-making that Singapore is. The national outpouring of grief following his death signalled how far Singapore has advanced as a nation since 1959. The question was — what type of nation should Singapore be? The realities of history, geography, demography, economic dependence and geopolitics drove Lee to carve a unique, tolerant multiracial nation through a policy of unity in diversity.

While this sounds rational and commonsensical today, in the 1950s and 1960s, it was revolutionary thinking. The easy option was to create a 'Chinese nation' in Singapore. This would have been tempting as the 1950s saw the rise of Chinese chauvinism and it would have been an easy strategy. Lee opposed this.

He opted for a much tougher route of galvanising everyone into the process of building a new nation as stakeholders, requiring Singaporeans to give up something and adopt new values of peaceful coexistence in a multiracial setting. He succeeded in imbuing a sense of attachment to Singapore, which is one of Mr Lee's lasting legacies.

National integration

Lee's success in defeating the communists in Singapore was particularly important in this endeavour. The communists played upon ethnic Chinese sentiments, championing Chinese education, language and culture. Lee knew that this was divisive internally and would also give the proximate neighbours an excuse to stymie Singapore's fledgling independence.

Following the victory of his People's Action Party (PAP) in the 1963 general election, after merger with Malaysia, Lee embarked on a bold experiment to transform Singapore, something that was pursued with greater vigour after independence on 9 August 1965. The crux of the experiment was aimed at creating social harmony and pursuit of policies that would promote economic growth in what was a highly divisive social terrain devoid of resources.

Many programmes were implemented to achieve these goals. The need to moderate racial, religious and linguistic demands was critical to ensure Singaporeans lived in harmony, especially after the 1964 racial riots. Ethnic, religious and linguistic identities were safeguarded to provide cultural ballast and accommodate the aspirations of a largely traditional Asian society. New national values were imbued with the principle of meritocracy determining social mobility and excellence in society.

Through subtle and robust measures, an integrated approach was adopted to transform the nation. This was undertaken through a plethora of policies in education, housing, national service, sharing of national economic wealth, job security, health care, efficient transport system, cleanliness, modern sanitation and provision of physical security. A nation emerged through good governance.

As nation-building is an emotional and psychological process, working on the 'heart-ware' was as important as hardware. It was about creating a new political consciousness. The ultimate aim was not just feeling good about Singapore but more importantly, feeling as Singaporeans. This involved a psychological mindset shift about believing in a Singaporean spirit.

Lee Kuan Yew's concept of nationhood

The death of Lee Kuan Yew and the unison of national grief expressed was a significant national political act. It symbolised shared values that he stood for, struggled against, championed and achieved. If Singapore collapses after Lee Kuan Yew, then the founder of modern Singapore would have failed. He imbued in the people a concept of nation, a spirit of never giving up, the value of national unity and the importance of success. He made Singaporeans realise that Singapore was a 'home', not a 'hotel'. With sustained successes on manifold fronts, the sense of national pride developed as Singapore came to symbolise the 'can-do' nation against all odds, in turn, cementing the sense of Singaporean Singapore.

While the physical transformation of Singapore from a swampy mudflat to a first world metropolis is self-evident, even more fundamental is Lee's success in creating a nation out of a potpourri of diverse immigrants from around Asia. This is a Singapore that enshrines values of harmony, incorruptibility, equal opportunity, hard work, excellence and above all, hopes for the future.

Lee Kuan Yew's dream of a great city-state, unique in history and where the people are not just people of Singapore but have learnt to embrace the world, will be one of his greatest legacies.

Singaporean Singapore — what next after Lee Kuan Yew?

The challenge for the next generation of political leaders and Singaporeans is how to ensure that the nation-in-being that was the handiwork of Lee Kuan Yew progresses upwards, not backwards. This is particularly challenging with the rise of ethno-nationalism and religious extremism worldwide, including in the geographical proximity of Singapore. The influx of foreigners into Singapore has also intensified this challenge.

The best practices of good governance and social interactions have informed Singaporeans that the roadmap laid down by the first generation of PAP leaders under Lee Kuan Yew's leadership will have to be even more robustly pursued and actualised. A nation based on the pre-eminence of any one ethnic group is a sure formula for national disaster, best manifested by experiences in Sri Lanka and Lebanon.

Lee's formula of nation-building has stood the test of time in recent history. The way ahead to manage national diversity is to embrace and not deny or manipulate it. Lee's Singapore has provided a model to manage all-round multiculturalism, not just for the outside world but even more important, for Singaporeans since 1965. This will be even more poignant in the post-Lee Kuan Yew era. The one principle that Lee embraced in leading Singapore was to give everyone under the Singapore Sun an equal place and hope for the future. It was all about realising the aspirations of what is enshrined in the National Anthem "*Majulah Singapura*" (Onward Singapore) and the National Pledge.

In post-LKY Singapore, nation-building challenges will become even more serious as pressures of globalisation, ethnic fault lines and new political issues emerge. As a new group of political leaders develop social compacts with the electorate — whatever transpires, the nation-building formula engineered by Lee Kuan Yew and his colleagues will become even more relevant as the alternative will be nation destruction. Singapore may be devoid of natural resources but through prudent policies, it has acquired a new powerful resource — national unity based on sound nation-building policies of a Singaporean Singapore. ∽

Bilveer Singh is an Associate Professor of Political Science at the National University of Singapore, and an Adjunct Senior Fellow at the Centre of Excellence for National Security (CENS), S. Rajaratnam School of International Studies (RSIS), Nanyang Technological University, Singapore.

Reviving Lee Kuan Yew's Legacy: Malay as the National Language

By Yang Razali Kassim

Synopsis

Of the immense and multi-faceted legacies of founding prime minister Lee Kuan Yew one which has not been sufficiently recognised is his introduction of Malay as the national language. What is its future role as Singapore forges to build a cohesive nation-state post-LKY?

Commentary

ON 11 AUGUST 1965 — two days after Singapore became independent, then-Prime Minister Lee Kuan Yew told a panel of journalists: "The pledge given by the People's Action Party (PAP) is not for the purposes of getting votes. We will earnestly carry it out. I make this promise: this is not a Chinese country. Singapore is not a Chinese country, nor a Malay country nor an Indian country..." Months later, speaking at the opening of a school on 19 December 1966, Lee added:

> *But to each also must be given the maximum of common denominators without which you and I will never be able to understand each other... And so it is we have designated that Malay should be our national language.*

It is significant that these two statements by Mr Lee were made after Singapore separated from Malaysia. In other words, the move to make Malay the national language was no longer driven by the political expediency of merger with Malaysia in 1963 but an expression of a new vision for an emergent nation-state; this new nation would be founded on a set of ideals detached from the hegemony of any one ethnic group yet unified by the symbolism of one of their languages. It was not to be Chinese, the language of the majority but Malay, the language of the biggest minority, as the national language. Hence soon after separation two years later, when the Singapore constitution was revised, the position of Malay as the national language was enshrined. This was in addition to its status as one of the four official languages — the others being Chinese, Tamil and English — with English as the working language.

Strategic masterstroke — Malay as national language

I would argue that of the immense and multi-faceted legacy of Lee Kuan Yew, the national language policy was one of the most strategic, and boldest by Singapore's first prime minister. It was also visionary, and a deft balancing act which only a leader of Lee's calibre could have pulled. Of Peranakan descent, he himself spoke Malay very well — which instantly drove home the point of a leader who meant what he said. He was also an English-educated Chinese, which meant he was serious about the majority not wielding hegemony over the minorities.

As a Peranakan, he was culturally and temperamentally well-placed to play the bridge-builder that the fledgling Singapore nation-state badly needed — between the various ethnic communities: the Chinese and the Malays and the Indians; and between the major linguistic gulfs, especially between the English-educated and the Chinese-educated.

His drive to create a new nation was so overpowering that he would compel the Chinese-educated not to push for Chinese to be the national language. This reflected his immense self-confidence in the demographic advantage that the Chinese majority enjoyed. And so over the following years, Malay, as the national language, would be sung as the national anthem, learned in schools, used in the uniformed services, even spoken by the Prime Minister — and his successors — during their annual State of the Nation addresses through the National Day Rallies (NDR). Whither the national language in the post-Lee Kuan Yew era?

Shifting ground

In the first 50 years of nationhood, the different ethnic groups adjusted fairly well to each other, although not without problems. For the minorities, this was a good start. In school, playing and studying together, they conversed in English, and occasionally for some, switched to simple, conversational Malay — giving rise to a sense of bonding. National service in the 1970s, their growing up years, saw Singaporeans from various races training together and marching to Malay commands. The cumulative impact was to imbibe a certain sense of solidarity among the trainees and a certain sense of localness — of being Singaporean. The environment was the same in university and in working life in the 1980s, although by then, English was decidedly the common tongue. The ability of friends and colleagues to converse in English and simple Malay sustained the feeling of togetherness. At work, Chinese-educated friends spoke with them in English and they enjoyed friendly banter in English.

But while Malay was the national language, the wide facility in English was the most important bridge across the ethnic and cultural divides. Everyone was speaking English — the Chinese, Malays, and Indians all sending their children to English schools. The Chinese, Malay and Tamil schools eventually closed down, primarily, under the weight of market forces.

English was also the social leveller as Singaporeans of every ethnic group spoke the language to get jobs and to communicate with each other in their respective ethnic twangs. Overtime, Singlish developed and surged to the forefront while Malay as the national language receded further into symbolism; there was a gradual but certain shift in the sociolinguistic landscape.

Since the 1990s, the shifting ground was apparent to the more discerning. Shopkeepers were either not able or not as easily inclined to break into conversational Malay. Taxi drivers were asking their passengers for destination in Singlish or English, and less in conversational Malay, unlike 10 years ago. Younger Singaporeans could be heard chatting away in Mandarin and not in English. In public places, such as in mass rapid transit (MRT) trains and malls, the chatter was as much in Mandarin as it was in English or Singlish.

While this was an understandable consequence of the changed education system, some were beginning to ask whether a gulf was emerging as a result of the generational shift. There was worry whether the different ethnic groups were drifting apart. Yet, at the same time, the national uniformed services — the military, police and civil defence — were still using the symbols of the national language, especially Malay, for their formation commands and drills, as vividly displayed during National Day parades. Significantly, the PM is still observing the language policy of using Malay, Mandarin and English, in that order, for his National Day Rally (NDR) speeches and the PAP's main party conferences, while Malay PAP Members of Parliament (MPs) also spoke Malay in parliamentary sessions.

Strangely, however, the announcers on television covering the NDRs would consistently refer to the PM delivering his 'speech in Malay', not 'speech in the national language' as it should rightly be. Some wondered whether this was a manifestation of oversight or ignorance, or more tellingly, of the widespread social amnesia of the fact that Malay is the national language.

Fortifying national identity amid changing demographics

While those who were quietly concerned about the perfunctory role of the national language were naturally Malays, over time this feeling was not the community's alone. A number of my non-Malay Singaporean friends were also noticing with equal concern, and they were not just from my generation but also younger ones. For example, I discovered that a friend from a local Chinese language newspaper was taking up Malay classes. Ironically, we were then travelling together on a conference trip to Beijing when she told me this. When I asked "Why?", she replied "Why not?" — "After all Malay is our national language," she said matter-of-factly.

This was a revelation for me — I had assumed, very wrongly, that a Singaporean from a Chinese-speaking environment would never feel any attachment with the national language. I wondered how many more Singaporeans were like her. If she was a reflection of a larger but unstated undercurrent of concern with regard to the state of the national language, then the future of social integration among Singapore's various communities in the next phase would be hopeful.

In more recent years, this concern was accentuated by the trend in immigration. As more and more foreigners took root in Singapore and became citizens as result of the government's open-door policy, how would they integrate and imbibe core Singaporean values and identity? Would they be able to understand the genesis and evolution of the Singaporean ethos, including multiracialism, and the reason for independent Singapore's founding fathers choosing Malay as the national language? A related concern was whether the changing demographics in Singapore, brought about by the growing immigration, would divide Singaporeans and hence, the need to bind themselves even more cohesively. It is in this context that the future role of the national language should be viewed.

Two years later, Kishore Mahbubani, one of Singapore's most influential public intellectuals, wrote a thought-provoking commentary in his Big Ideas column in *The Straits Times*. On 14 June 2014, his 'Big Idea No. 5: Speak the National Language' called for a campaign to revive the national language by encouraging Singaporeans to speak Bahasa Melayu (the Malay Language). His comment was unprecedented in its openness, frankness and clarity of message. I could not recall any public figure, Malay or non-Malay, who so cogently and boldly made such an exhortation. He said, "Please notice I did not say 'study' the national language. Nor did I say 'read' or 'write' the national language. I only said 'speak' because we should set a very low bar and get most Singaporeans connected with their national language."

He listed five reasons, "in ascending order of importance why Singaporeans should learn to speak Bahasa Melayu": The first is to be a normal country because Singapore was to him an "abnormal country" as most Singaporeans do not speak their national language. Second, Singaporeans would be able to sing their national anthem with greater feeling and passion if they knew a few words of Bahasa Melayu. Third is the pragmatic reason of being surrounded by Malay-speaking neighbours such as Malaysia, Indonesia and Brunei. The ability to speak the same language would open up various opportunities, including economic ones.

Besides, by 2030, according to one projection he cited, Indonesia may become the seventh-largest economy in the world, overtaking Britain and Germany. The fourth reason is a geopolitical one — "Most small nations survive over the longer term by developing geopolitical understanding of the neighbourhood." The final reason, "and perhaps the most important reason for speaking Bahasa Melayu", he said, "is that a common understanding of our national language will be one more invisible thread that will make our nation a more cohesive one".

What next?

It is interesting to note how Professor Kishore's call was received by Singaporeans who have essentially grown up not being familiar with the national language, apart from singing the national anthem. At the same time, the rise of China and the consequent growing importance of Mandarin has confirmed the foresight of Lee Kuan Yew promoting the learning of Mandarin among Chinese Singaporeans. Against this backdrop, it is not surprising if sections of Singaporean society viewed the learning of Chinese as a "pragmatic step" in view of China's growing influence. Yet, it could be argued that it is for this same reason that it becomes compelling to remind Singaporeans of who they are as Singaporeans first and foremost. It is also precisely due to the potential uncertainties of the next 50 years that there is a need for a centripetal pull towards the centre — a pull which the national language is best poised for and should play.

Significantly, there appears also to be resonance among non-Malay Singaporeans who supported Kishore's urging for the revival of Malay as the national language. For instance, on 24 November 2014, *The Straits Times* ran a letter by Jong Ching Yee calling on Singaporeans to pick up Malay as a third conversational language for social interaction in Singapore's multiracial society and as a link with the region.

Echoing Jong's call, Paul Sim Ruiqi, writing in the same forum page, called for learning of the national language as a bridge to a deeper understanding of local history and culture. Taking this call further in 2014, another reader, Lee Yong Se, called on the Government to promote the revival of the national language and to ride on the momentum of Singapore's 50th anniversary celebrations to do this: "As we celebrate SG50 next year, my wish is that more non-Malay Singaporeans, especially new citizens, would be well-versed in the national language."

This growing realisation of the unifying role of the national language was noted by the Government. Speaking at the launch of the Malay Language Month for 2014, Deputy Prime Minister Tharman Shanmugaratnam said:

> *"Malay is our national language and the Malay culture is a part of our common heritage and identity."*

Reviving the national language — Role of government and Malay community

So what can be done? To begin with, there is a need for a study on the thinking of Singaporeans, after 50 years of independence, on how the national language can be better positioned in the next phase of Singapore's evolution as a nation-state. In this context, there are three key determining factors: national society, the Government and the Malay community.

There will come a time when Singaporeans will feel the void, or to paraphase Kishore's statement, the "abnormality" of Singapore where there is a national language but the people do not speak it. To many, this situation has arisen due to the lack of active government policy to promote the national language, quite apart from retaining it in symbolic form at the parade square, at NDRs or PAP general assemblies. Views from the ground have indeed emerged on the way forward. One Straits Times reader, Roland Seow, responding to Kishore's call, proposed to "bring back Bahasa Melayu as a subject in school" while another, Alan Kiong, appealed to "please make this a national policy". Bringing back the national language is clearly a major exercise in uplifting the national spirit. As Wong Wee Nam wrote in Sgpolitics.net in 2011:

"There must be a conscious attempt to promote the national language. People must be reminded that there is a national language."

The Malay community must also play its part. The national language must be kept alive among young Malay Singaporeans in the face of the community's increasing adaptation and growing use of English. Going forward, the importance of the national language must be reflected in the community as the living embodiment of the national language. Malay Singaporeans must see their own use of the national language as their contribution to the organic growth of a multi-ethnic Singaporean Singapore. I see no contradiction in this — the more Malay is used as the national language, the more Singaporean we become. As the country's indigenous people, the Malays are also the living reminder of Singapore's pre-Raffles past, centuries ago as a dynamic trading post — much like today — when Malay was the regional lingua franca.

The revival of the national language as the glue for a 21st century Singapore provides the continuity amid change that Prime Minister Lee Hsien Loong so vividly talked about when he envisioned recently the future Singaporean nation-state 50 years hence. At this major crossroads of nationhood, Lee Kuan Yew's formula of always maintaining the fine strategic balance, a formula that he has bequeathed to the Singaporean nation-state, must survive him — as much internally as externally on the international stage.

EPILOGUE: *ON 23 AUGUST 2015, Prime Minister Lee Hsien Loong delivered his National Day Rally speech, coinciding with SG50 — the celebration marking the 50th anniversary of Singapore's independence. As usual, he spoke in three languages; beginning with Malay, followed by Mandarin and finally in English for his main delivery. This time however, Mr Lee preambled his address in a way that he, or any other prime minister, had never done before. "This year's rally is special... We are looking back on 50 years of nation-building and also looking forward to many more years of progress. Let me begin in our national language." Switching to Malay, he said: "Biar saya mulakan dalam Bahasa Kebangsaan kita." (Let me begin in our national language). In his NDR speech a year earlier in 2014, he prefaced his three addresses by saying "Let me begin first in Malay, as usual." This linguistic shift is subtle but significant. In so doing, the Prime Minister had re-emphasised the centrality of the national language, coming as it did at a crucial juncture in nationhood. In another development two days later, on 25 August 2015, the 2015 general election was called for 11 September 2015. During the hustings, a handful of candidates from both the ruling People's Action Party (PAP) and the Opposition spoke in Malay, other than their main languages English and Mandarin. One key non-Malay opposition candidate, Gerald Giam from the Workers' Party, specifically mentioned that he would be speaking "dalam Bahasa Kebangsaan" (in the national language).* 🎗

Yang Razali Kassim is a Senior Fellow with the S. Rajaratnam School of International Studies (RSIS), Nanyang Technological University, Singapore. He is also the Editor of RSIS Commentary as well as Strategic Currents. An earlier version of this appeared in the National University of Singapore Society's publication NUSS Commentary: Singapore@50 Reflections and Observations.

Singapore's Strategic Future: Lee Kuan Yew's Legacy for the Next 50 Years

By Mushahid Ali

Synopsis

With the passing of Singapore's founding prime minister Lee Kuan Yew, what will the future hold for Singapore? How will this tiny island nation fare over the next five decades?

Commentary

WHEN SINGAPORE seceded from Malaysia on 9 August 1965, it embarked on a hazardous course to survive on its own, an unlikely nation in an unfriendly environment. Undeterred by the conflicts and wars raging in Southeast Asia, Lee Kuan Yew steered his tiny ship of state to an uncertain future with a strategic vision and steely resolve to make it an oasis of peace, prosperity and stability in an unpromising region.

Cast adrift from its natural hinterland and bereft of its traditional role of an entrepôt between East Asia and Western Europe, Singapore sought a new footing as a business hub in international trade and global communications network, leveraging on its strategic location at the maritime crossroads of the Indo-Pacific oceans and potential aviation transiting point between Eurasia and Australasia.

What does the future hold for Singapore?

His guiding principle was to make Singapore relevant to the rest of the world and thereby give the world powers a stake in the continued survival and security of Singapore. That principle has been the bedrock of Singapore's strategy for the past 50 years as it embarked on an ambitious programme of economic development through industrialisation; communications and logistical upgrading; high technology engineering and manufacturing; petrochemical and pharmaceutical research and development; defence and knowledge-based industries; and educational and financial services. It was a vision of a strategic future that the population of Singapore bought into and adopted as their own.

What does the future hold for Singapore? Will it be still independent and sovereign or become part of a bigger entity? Still prosperous and thriving or reduced to penury by circumstances beyond its control? In short, what is the strategic future of Singapore in the next 50 years? Can the strategic vision of Lee Kuan Yew serve Singapore well in the next 50 years?

It should. Singapore's progress in the next five decades will need to build on its achievements of the last 50 years and adapt its capabilities to meet the challenges the new era will bring — globalisation, a more open and possibly internet-connected trading arrangement, and technological revolution. Singapore will need to continue to make itself relevant and an integral part of the global supply chain economy, as a financial centre and logistics node.

To overcome limitations of space and size, Singapore has to continue expanding its economic space by extending its wings in China and India and consolidating its economic integration with its ASEAN neighbours, quantitatively and qualitatively, through the ASEAN Community and the Asia-Pacific Economic Cooperation (APEC), which Singapore has been jointly instrumental in creating. Singapore will need to extend its economic linkages with Asia and beyond to meet the expected competition and contestation of its role from neighbouring countries.

Extrapolating its experience in producing trained manpower for the new economy, Singapore will help in the higher education and training of the younger generation of ASEAN citizens, thereby enlarging the pool of skilled manpower for its economic development. Singapore should continue to help build new urban centres in China, India and mainland ASEAN and develop ports and communications centres in maritime ASEAN and South Asia, thereby enhancing its geopolitical relevance and linkages with the Asia–Pacific region.

Pivotal fulcrum in balance of power

Singapore has to maintain its exceptional geopolitical space in a changing global architecture as the Indo-Pacific region becomes the cockpit of contention of the new superpowers — China, India, America and Europe. Even as the balance of power of the Indo-Pacific region shifts with the inexorable rise of China, the military growth of India and Japan, coupled with the rebalancing of the United States to the Western Pacific, Singapore will maintain its geo-strategic position as a pivotal fulcrum of the region.

That role will be buttressed by its strategic partnerships with the US and other major powers, along with defence and military cooperation with Australia, India, Japan and other medium powers. Inevitably it will strike up a strategic partnership with China, which will become a significant contributor to the security and stability of the Asia Pacific. As Lee Kuan Yew saw it, in any configuration of the major powers, Singapore has to ensure that it has the superior lineup of forces on its side.

Having built its capacity for defence and security the past five decades, Singapore should increase its defence cooperation with its ASEAN neighbours while upgrading its joint exercises with major powers such as the United States, Australia, India and Japan, to face possible threats to their security from non-state actors and non-traditional sources such as transnational terrorist groups, natural disasters and climate change.

In short, Singapore has to enhance its relevance and usefulness in regional and international security arrangements, such as providing facilities for coordinated air and naval patrols; humanitarian and disaster relief; and countering transnational crime and terrorism. In effect, Singapore has to expand its role as a regional centre for information fusion, and logistics for anti-piracy and disaster relief, and become the operational headquarters for ASEAN defence cooperation as well as a key logistics base for an Asia-Pacific security network involving like-minded powers such as Australia, Japan and India as well as China.

Singapore as spearhead of regional connectivity

Singapore should be in the forefront of efforts to enhance connectivity among ASEAN and Indo-Pacific countries, by land, sea and air, and play a major role in facilitating Indonesia's Maritime Fulcrum objective as well as China's Maritime Silk Route. In sum, Singapore should continue to be the communications and strategic hub of Southeast Asia and the Asia-Pacific.

In the socio-cultural field, Singapore should become the centre of performing arts of ASEAN while promoting its own hybrid culture melding Asian and Western traditions, and energising the rejuvenation of the art, dance, music and literature of the ASEAN countries.

To overcome its physical constraints, Singapore can expand its working and living space by enlarging economic cooperation with Malaysia and Indonesia through joint investments in their economic corridors such as Iskandar Malaysia and the Riau Archipelago, thereby anchoring Singapore in the growth triangles of the two neighbours.

Singapore will still maintain its sovereignty while becoming interdependent with and integrating in an economic configuration with Indonesia and Malaysia that will secure the strategic future of this island state — for the next 50 years and beyond. ℘

Mushahid Ali is a Senior Fellow with the S. Rajaratnam School of International Studies (RSIS), Nanyang Technological University, Singapore.

Leaving a Lasting Legacy

By Toh Ting Wei

Synopsis

One of Lee Kuan Yew's many legacies is the birth of Nanyang Technological University. In this essay published by the campus newspaper, Nanyang Chronicle, two of NTU's former presidents recall the first prime minister's impact on them.

Mr Lee Kuan Yew's final appearance in NTU, in a dialogue with students on 5 September 2011, moderated by Associate Provost (Student Life) Kwok Kian Woon. Photo by courtesy of The Straits Time © Singapore Press Holdings, reprinted with permission.

Commentary

"If not for Mr Lee Kuan Yew, there will be no NTU." These were Professor Cham Tao Soon's first words to the Nanyang Chronicle in an interview on 31 March 2015, a week after the passing of Singapore's first prime minister on 23 March 2015.

The founding president of the university readily pointed out that he would not have had the opportunity to take up the position, had the late Mr Lee not made the decision to merge the old Nanyang University (Nantah) with the then-University of Singapore back in 1980.

LKY's strong hand behind NTU

Professor Cham said: "One of his legacies is actually the creation of NTU. After the merger went through, one of his three promises was to provide a better university in return. The promises he made then were possible to fulfil, but it required a lot of effort."

While Mr Lee's contributions to Singapore have been well documented, less known is the fact that he also had a strong hand in NTU's growth from Nantah to Nanyang Technological Institute, before its evolution into NTU today.

Nantah, NTU's predecessor, was a Chinese-medium university that experienced strong support from the Chinese community — but a declining graduate employment, and the decreasing value of a Nantah degree had prompted concerns about the future of the university.

Then-Prime Minister, Mr Lee had pushed through a merger of the University of Singapore and Nantah to form the National University of Singapore, to address the issue.

Apart from promising to provide a better university following the merger of Nantah, Mr Lee also made two other promises: to use the old Nantah campus and retain the name Nanyang, and to turn the campus into a full fledged university in 10 years. These promises all rested on the shoulders of Professor Cham, who successfully fulfilled them.

"The success of NTU was very important to him (as it would prove) that he was right. It was not easy to close down a Chinese-medium university supported by the local Chinese community, who formed about 80 per cent of the population then."

"Hence, he had to make sure it was successful from a political perspective," Professor Cham said.

Having made the promise of replacing Nantah with a better university, Mr Lee kept a keen eye on NTU's development in its formative years. As a result, a friendship developed between him and Professor Cham, with the two having about 50 lunches together. This took place on a monthly basis, over a period of five years between 1988 to 1992.

"Mr Lee would drop in (to visit NTU) unannounced on weekends, and a week later he would drop me a note with suggestions. In terms of helping me out, he was a very persistent man," said Professor Cham.

Among Mr Lee's suggestions to improve the NTU campus was the building of sheltered walkways, an idea he came up with while he was on one of his incognito weekend visits to NTU.

Professor Cham pointed out that NTU's investment in landscaping then was influenced by Mr Lee's passion for greenery, with Mr Lee even making suggestions for the canopy on campus.

"He did not put pressure on me, and has always given me a lot of assistance."

"Even during our lunches together, we hardly discussed education," said Professor Cham. He noted that the drive to succeed at NTU stemmed from pressure placed on himself.

NTU, geopolitics and key events

In his book *The Making of NTU — My Story*, Professor Cham credited the lunches with Mr Lee as the reason for NTU forming partnerships with other international institutions.

He stated: "Geopolitics, Singapore's place in global affairs and the key events — all these were analysed and given Mr Lee's particular touch. It was because I was armed with this wisdom that I began NTU's venture into partnerships and organisations all over the world."

While Mr Lee's involvement in NTU had reduced by the time Professor Cham stood down as NTU President in December 2002, his impact was still felt by Professor Cham's successor, Professor Su Guaning.

Professor Su, who helmed NTU from 2003 to 2011, noted that with NTU focused on advancing its research capabilities by the time he took over, Mr Lee's support for then-Deputy Prime Minister Dr Tony Tan — who was spearheading NTU's drive on research — proved to be invaluable.

"Dr Tan made it possible for us to make the next leap into a research-intensive global university that was ranked highly globally, through creating this autonomous university framework (which reduced bureaucratic red tape when making decisions) and starting the National Research Foundation."

"I am almost sure that he would have to go through Mr Lee for this, because he needed to convince the whole cabinet that it was important for Singapore," Professor Su told the Chronicle in an interview on 26 March.

"The decision to become an autonomous university was the most important one. Politically, the tradition since independence has been to keep a close watch on universities. So when Dr Tan proposed the framework of an autonomous university to the Cabinet then, I am pretty sure he must have had the support of Mr Lee. Without his support, it would have been difficult to convince the rest of the Cabinet," Professor Su added.

Personal touch

While Mr Lee's decisions have had lasting impact on NTU, he has also left deep impressions on some members of the NTU community.

Among them was Mrs Hazel Loh, now Deputy Director and Head of Library Technology & Systems Group. A young librarian back in the late 1980s, she was assigned to deliver a briefing to Mr Lee on an informal visit to NTU's library.

Ms Loh, who was in her twenties then, said: "I was very excited, and felt it was such a rare honour to be selected by my boss to do a briefing for Mr Lee, who was the PM at that time."

"He came across as a fatherly figure with such a nice rosy complexion. He also had a warm disposition and showed interest in what I was saying during the briefing."

"With so many important areas to take care of as Prime Minister, I felt he had an interest in people to have made an effort to visit the different parts of the campus and not just meet with the key administration."

In contrast, Professor Cham was far from excited prior to his very first lunch meeting with Mr Lee back in 1988.

He said: "I was very nervous the first time I met him for lunch. He had a reputation of being very forceful and stern, and I thought he was a critical man. But he turned out to be a very good host."

Professor Cham pointed out that all the meetings he had with Mr Lee left deep impressions on him, especially with Mr Lee's thought process and long-term vision. One quote, which has stuck with him till this day, was the late Prime Minister's thoughts on Singapore's prospects.

"I asked him how he saw Singapore's future, and his view is that it is a small country with little needs, so he sees no problem if everyone works hard, barring world disasters."

"Even though he was a bit worried about the younger generation who have never gone through any hardship before, it is reassuring to know that he thinks we will be alright if we work hard," said Professor Cham.

While Professor Su did not have any personal anecdotes to share, Mr Lee's contributions to Singapore still left a lasting impression on him. Hailing him as an irreplaceable figure, Professor Su noted that "history would judge him kindly together with his founding team".

He concluded: "All in all, I think even those who are very much opposed to his policies in some aspects do hold great respect for him for bringing Singapore to where we are today. Even those whom Mr Lee would see as his enemies would applaud him, so I think that is a wonderful achievement on his part." ∞

Toh Ting Wei was News Editor of the Nanyang Chronicle where this essay first appeared. This is a campus newspaper published by Wee Kim Wee School of Communication and Information (WKWSCI), Nanyang Technological University, Singapore.

What Lee Kuan Yew Means to Youth Today

By Ang Hwee Min & Lo Yi Min

Synopsis

As Singaporeans reel from the loss of their first prime minister and founding father of independent Singapore, some reflect on what Mr Lee Kuan Yew means to Singapore's youth of today.

Commentary

SINGAPORE'S FIRST Prime Minister Lee Kuan Yew is widely regarded as a significant contributor to the nation's development. Unsurprisingly, his passing on 23 March 2015 spurred the sharing of many eulogies. They took different forms and came from varied sources, including international newspapers; Mr Lee's own son, Prime Minister Lee Hsien Loong, and other family members; and ordinary Singaporeans whose lives have been touched by the man.

Tributes online include Instagram dedications and Facebook status updates, with hashtags such as #RememberingLKY and #thankYew being used to track posts. Articles posted on the social media accounts of news outlets were shared

149

over and over again, their discussion threads bursting at the seams.

Hopping on the tribute bandwagon?

Among the dedication posts, a few went especially viral, including a portrait of the late Mr Lee by local artist Ong Yi Teck, 20, created through hand-writing the former's full name 18,000 times. In light of the deluge of messages on social media sites honouring Mr Lee's achievements and all he has done for Singapore, it was easy for many to write off the posts as watered-down and superficial, or even attention-seeking — as much of the content found online can be.

In their online eulogies, many of the more adventurous and tech-savvy youth paid tribute to his legacy by penning verses of grandeur on Facebook and artistically composed, carefully filtered photographs on Instagram. Just as quickly, many criticised the supposedly shallow method of eulogising, asserting that the outpouring of affection and gratitude was merely a sign of a generation being washed along by collective grief.

Eventually, however, the ever understanding public decided that hopping on the tribute bandwagon was merely natural — coming from a generation with purportedly little attachment to a political figure none of them had the chance to grow up directly under.

Changing tides

As a generation who has only heard of the Third World port Singapore used to be, the youth of today may be chided for blindly bequeathing a founding father with overflowing gratitude and reverence. However, in retrospect, perhaps the appreciation shown demonstrates that national identity lies beyond how our nation is built.

Grounding our impressions of Mr Lee in his private life further magnifies the respect Singapore holds for him. Seeing Mr Lee as more than the man who — with the help of others — cultivated our nation strengthens the narrative that appreciates the value of his leadership.

It adds meaning to our collective history, and possibly gives the youth of today enough depth to resolve themselves from some measure of distaste that others have pressed upon them.

But as tears fell along with the heavy torrential downpour on the morning of Mr Lee's state funeral procession, it can be said that this is a generation that has inherited the capacity to examine its roots with nuanced understanding.

A Mandarin idiom goes: *"When you drink water, think of its source."*

Let it not be said that the youth of today are grateful for all the wrong reasons. To be able to learn from what we know of Mr Lee Kuan Yew outside of his political life shows that Singapore's narrative is ready to sail on to its next chapter, one beyond the shadow of his legacy.

Initial impressions

Yet, it must be acknowledged that the lack of first-hand experience does not and should not prevent the said generation from appreciating the far-reaching influence of the man who shaped Singapore into the city they live in. This behaviour resembles a verse in Walt Whitman's "Song of Myself". The American poet wrote in his famous poem: "You will hardly know who I am or what I mean. But I shall be good health to you nevertheless, and filter and fibre your blood."

Generations that came after the late Mr Lee relinquished his post as Prime Minister have never directly encountered his brash, no-nonsense governance. However, they have certainly learnt of the man with "iron in him" who has kept the body of Singapore in good health.

Finding himself a place in politics, the Cambridge-educated lawyer led the transformation of a newly-independent nation from a port city populated by migrants to the thriving metropolis we are now, through pragmatic policies often described as "authoritative" by Western media. His heavy-handed leadership remains salient in the minds of international critics.

This style of governance in the founding years of post-independence Singapore appear to reflect the qualities of our first Prime Minister himself, a view cemented by national discourse and many textbooks. In an article published on the website of *The Guardian* on 23 March 2015 titled "Lee Kuan Yew Leaves a Legacy of Authoritarian Pragmatism", the author wrote that Mr Lee "moulded Singapore in his own image", which resulted in what our nation is today.

Mr Lee's Cabinet policies have shaped us as a pragmatic yet idealistic nation, blessing us with advantages like bilingualism, clean streets, and successful public housing plans. From photogenic Housing Development Board (HDB) flats to challenging Mother Tongue lessons, the youth of Singapore today have only experienced the fruits of his labour, without seeing Singaporeans of the yesteryear toiling for survival.

Filling in the blanks

Despite not knowing much of the specific details on how and what he did for our country, one cannot escape the resurfacing of these narratives in public discourse since his passing. Singaporeans who came after his time as Prime Minister also happen to be the ones most exposed to social media sites. ⁏

Ang Hwee Min and Lo Yi Min are Opinions Editors of the Nanyang Chronicle, a campus newspaper published by the Wee Kim Wee School of Communication and Information (WKWSCI), Nanyang Technological University, Singapore, where this article first appeared.

Singapore's Future Post-LKY: What Do Young Singaporeans Want?

By Nur Diyanah Anwar

Synopsis

Singapore's economic success and multiracial harmony has largely been attributed to the leadership of founding prime minister Lee Kuan Yew. However, with current complexities confronting Singapore's governance, would his passing necessarily mark a change in Singapore's future trajectory? What is the role of young Singaporeans?

Commentary

SINGAPORE'S INTERNATIONAL regard as an economically successful and multiracial society belies the concerns many Singaporeans may have about the resilience of Singapore in today's globalised and competitive world. A younger, more vocal and educated populace equipped with advanced technology find it easier to air their opinions on various issues concerning Singapore publicly, compared to previous generations of Singaporeans.

While Singapore currently celebrates multiracial harmony and a first-world status — largely attributed to its first prime minister Lee Kuan Yew — there is an increasing sense of dissatisfaction amongst some Singaporeans which may affect efforts to build a more cohesive Singapore society. Would Mr Lee's passing necessarily mark a change in Singapore's trajectory into the future?

Post-LKY — What does this mean?

The passing of a personality as defining as Lee Kuan Yew would inevitably call into question the future of the country without him. Would Singapore survive him? There is currently an undercurrent of discontent among some in the populace towards the government — especially young Singaporeans — over issues such as the availability of jobs for citizens, and the influx of foreigners into Singapore. This highlights the changing fabric and character of the Singapore society, which may only grow more complex for governance today.

It would, however, be naïve to assume Singapore would change drastically post-LKY. The current prime minister, Lee Hsien Loong, mentioned during the 7th ASEAN Journalists Visit Programme that "in the last 15 years, it is a new team which has been taking Singapore, making the decisions, carrying them, persuading people or dealing with problems when they have risen". There is, nonetheless, a need to address the dissatisfaction present within the populace to improve the quality of governance in the country and sustain a cohesive society.

To this end, surviving Lee Kuan Yew would essentially mean to continue Singapore's impressive trajectory into the future and embracing his foresight. The true test for Singapore post-LKY is to adapt to and address any concerns within a changing environment, while learning from the lessons he had left behind for Singaporeans. Surviving Lee Kuan Yew in today's climate of dissatisfaction would mean for current (and future) leaders to continually review their policies and communication approaches to regain the trust of the public, especially the younger generation.

Upholding LKY's pragmatism

A potent lesson many Singaporeans can identify with from Lee Kuan Yew's leadership is his emphasis on pragmatism. This largely entails focusing on outcomes in the best interest of Singapore when solving problems concerning the country — to do what he regarded was right and not what was popular. He understood the extent of Singapore's vulnerabilities, and addressed each obstacle with practicality — ensuring that each solution was feasible and sustainable enough to meet Singapore's needs into the future.

Such pragmatism can be observed through the policies implemented under his premiership from the early post-independence years till he stepped down in 1990. These policies — such as those on housing, meritocracy and education, and an emphasis on an incorruptible government and public service — can prove to be his lasting legacy as they embodied the very essence of pragmatism for the Singapore society at large.

For example, housing policies were aimed at instilling communitarianism. Housing quotas designed to promote inter-ethnic mixing in housing block flats were placed to encourage tolerance and good relations amongst neighbours. This ended the concentrations of ethnic groups living in enclaves, which would not have been good for national integration in the long-term. Ultimately, housing ownership fostered a sense of pride by giving each citizen a stake in Singapore.

Secondly, Lee Kuan Yew aligned education in Singapore with the principle of meritocracy. This philosophy rewards the deserving with economic success and social mobility, ensuring equal opportunities for all regardless of race or religion. This not only reinforced self-reliance and hardwork among the working and studying populations, but also built the foundations upon which Singaporeans pride themselves as a meritocratic society.

Thirdly, Mr Lee's practical emphasis on an incorruptible government and public service has been well-noted internationally. He ensured that a clean and trustworthy government should lead the public service by example, where such ethical behaviour would be translated throughout society. Such pragmatism has benefitted Singapore; Singapore's incorruptibility has set itself apart and continues to instil investor confidence and political stability.

It would be worth noting that these policies were largely borne out of a period when Singapore had still experienced inter-racial tensions amid the restructuring of a fledgling economy in the 1960s and 1970s. They however crystallised

Lee Kuan Yew's foresight in giving Singaporeans some fundamental characteristics to live by — traits which have eventually contributed to Singapore's continuous growth and stability. Pragmatism should therefore continue to be the beacon guiding Singapore post-LKY.

What should we expect post-LKY?

The question that should instead be asked is if Singapore's leadership is ready to take on a more open and dialectic governance model post-LKY. This is to manage the latent sense of dissatisfaction amongst some Singaporeans which may hinder a cohesive Singapore society while reducing the hierarchical distance between the leaders and Singaporeans. While such consensual governance has arguably been attempted — from the likes of "Our Singapore Conversation" and through platforms such as REACH (Reaching Everyone for Active Citizenry@Home) — it is not enough to satisfy younger Singaporeans who may not be shy to critique, especially on social media platforms.

Discussions between Singaporeans and the leaders should not be used to merely justify government decisions, as Singaporeans may not be able to fully grasp the practicalities and realities behind them in the first place. However, young Singaporeans would like to discuss beyond the superficial; they would like to be engaged in deeper conversations, and be respected for their opinions at the table.

As such, greater efforts should be made to reach out further to this section of the population so that the leadership remains relevant to them. A softer form of pragmatism here would test the capacity of the leadership's governance and its adaptability to changes in the society, while keeping to the lessons that Singapore has been built upon from Lee Kuan Yew. In this regard, the opinions of the young, educated and technologically-savvy Singaporeans should be seriously taken into consideration for Singapore's development in the years ahead. It should focus on gaining the trust of the younger generation in Singapore's governance.

Pragmatism, therefore, should continue to be a cornerstone of Singapore's governance and society. Surviving Lee Kuan Yew in today's climate of disaffection amongst young Singaporeans would require continual review of the policy and communication approaches used in governance, and bringing the opinions of young Singaporeans more prominently into the equation. This can contribute to Singapore's trajectory into the future with greater success, and possibly assuage any concern Singaporeans may have about the state of the society in today's globalised and competitive world. 🙾

Nur Diyanah Anwar is a Research Analyst with the Centre of Excellence for National Security (CENS), S. Rajaratnam School of International Studies (RSIS), Nanyang Technological University, Singapore.

Will There Be Another LKY?

By Dylan Loh

Synopsis

Lee Kuan Yew's legacy to Singapore is immense and manifold spanning several decades. What do young Singaporeans who have not lived through his leadership think of his ideas?

Commentary

LEE KUAN YEW has been called many things: "visionary leader", "hatchet man", "intellectual giant", and of course, "founding father of modern Singapore". One aspect of the founding prime minister that has largely escaped this discourse, however, is his influence on young Singaporeans — especially those who did not live under his stewardship of Singapore through the heady and traumatic days of self-government, merger and independence.

This perspective of Lee Kuan Yew, stripped of the historical burden of that period, is by one young Singaporean who has not experienced his *tour de force* in its entirety; it is by one of those born in the 1980s when Singapore's founding father dominated the state's governance.

Lee Kuan Yew's impact on young Singaporeans

There are several key differences in how the younger generation view Lee Kuan Yew compared to the older generation. For one, young people do not view him as deeply as those who have lived through his leadership and his administration. It is, therefore, much harder for younger Singaporeans to relate to both the substance and style of governance of Lee Kuan Yew. That is not to say younger Singaporeans do not admire his style of leadership. Certainly, there seems to be a yearning of sorts, however unpractical (or practical) it may be, for the kinds of selflessness and dedication demonstrated by him and his team. That much is clear from the outpouring of grief and emotion during his passing, especially, among younger Singaporeans.

It would be impossible to map out all the significant legacies Lee Kuan Yew left behind. Rather, the focus will be on just two ideational legacies which had a substantial impact on my generation. To be sure, his steadfast belief in pragmatism must be one of the most important normative gifts to the nation. One ideational legacy Lee Kuan Yew left behind is the notion of the nation's vulnerability.

He once said: "To understand Singapore, you've got to start off with an improbable story: It should not exist." This was a brilliant concept that is, by and large, accepted by younger Singaporeans. It is brilliant in the sense that it underpins and justifies many other ideas and, indeed, substantive policies taken under the name of 'vulnerability'. His favourite question was not "Is this right?", but "So what?"

This 'so what' question removes grand narratives and the idealism of morality but rather, brings into focus whether taking a course of action benefits or protects Singapore's interests. Indeed, he eschews grand theories or ideals and is guided by what benefits Singapore most. "Does it work? Let's try it and if it does work, fine, let's continue it. If it doesn't work, toss it out, try another one," he said. This 'siege mentality' is especially pronounced in regard to Singapore's existence and its security outlook and foreign affairs.

Of course, there are increasingly more questions posed on this 'vulnerability' meme, challenging its accuracy. Many of these are valid questions. However, certain existential realities cannot simply be challenged away — the smallness of size; the almost non-existent natural resources; and more significantly, the problematic fall in birth rates. In international relations, it similarly follows that its smallness limits its flexibility to manoeuvre.

Singapore simply does not have the latitude that many larger countries enjoy and that meant it had to invest heavily in defence and make its foreign affairs first-rate.

Beyond state vulnerability, the idea of being vulnerable has profound effects on individual young Singaporeans and this notion manifests itself very clearly in education and in the workforce. To that end, Lee Kuan Yew once said: "We never went for an iron rice bowl. Each person has his own porcelain rice bowl. And if you break it — it's your bad luck. And you look after it, when it is porcelain."

Myth or not, the idea of constantly being vulnerable creates a benign form of paranoia which pushes us to be exceptional just to survive. Examples are aplenty showing the grit, productivity and tenacity of young Singaporeans to build a "rugged society" rendering depictions of the younger generation as a 'strawberry generation', as being 'soft' or 'weak,' somewhat exaggerated.

Singaporean exceptionalism?

Next, and closely coupled with the first idea, is that of 'Singaporean exceptionalism'. This is distinctly different from 'American exceptionalism' in the vein of 'manifest destiny' or even Chinese exceptionalism. This is not a belief in the narrative that we are special and we are great but, once again informed by the vulnerability leitmotif, a belief that we need to strive to be exceptional as individuals and as a nation to survive and to stay relevant.

This may also hold true for older Singaporeans but, then again, they were, generally more occupied with making ends meet, not being 'exceptional' in that sense. What this meant for our generation is that we tend to work very hard — Singaporeans clock one of the longest working hours, globally, according to several polls — and constantly attempt to acquire new knowledge to stay relevant and to be ahead of the curve.

Collectively, Singapore has found multiple niches on the global stage which makes it important enough to matter.

For example, Singapore is a leader in the finance and services industry and remains one of the few countries in the world to have a triple 'A' credit rating from all the top three credit rating agencies. Clearly, this did not happen by serendipity or happenstance; it was planned, engineered and worked at to maintain our competitive edge — our exceptional standing. Besides that, Singapore students consistently rank as one of the best in the world, as do our universities.

While the unintended consequence is that this breeds a culture that favours middle and upper-class families and creates students who are 'exam-smart', nevertheless, the spirit and ideal of always trying to be exceptional is a positive one. For me, the idea of striving to be exceptional to stay on par or survive is very real and has certainly influenced me and how I see Singapore.

Challenges going forward: Three difficult questions

There are many challenges going forward, collectively, in a post-Lee Kuan Yew era. Many of these are already being discussed and debated. I would, however, bring to attention three 'questions' a young Singaporean may ask, to which there are no easy answers.

The first is whether we can, or indeed should, we find the next 'Lee Kuan Yew'? While we lament the loss of the man gone by, we frequently think that for another 'Lee Kuan Yew' to emerge is almost impossible. We cite the uniqueness of his character and circumstances for the making of the man and resign ourselves that Lee Kuan Yew was a one-off event. If so, are we content with having many good leaders over a few exceptional men or women? Or perhaps the next 'Lee Kuan Yew' of Singapore, ironically, should not be like him at all. Perhaps in answering these questions, we need to take a hard (although admittedly uncomfortable) look at 'meritocracy' and how we identify and groom future leaders of Singapore.

The second question is "what is the vision for the next 50 years?" With Lee Kuan Yew, that vision was clear. Even after his gradual retirement from politics, he was able to articulate in very succinct and evocative ways what he thought Singapore ought to be. Post-Lee Kuan Yew, are we able to craft a vision of Singapore in the next 10 to 50 years that will excite, convince and galvanise us? For people my age, the next few decades would be the most productive years of our lives and we yearn for a compelling and inspiring vision that would tap on those productive energies.

Finally, despite our great work to create niches, we worry if we will be swept away by the tides of great power competition. Without a great Asian statesman, will Singapore's expert views still be sought? Would the diplomatic and political goodwill Lee Kuan Yew accrued be expended wastefully or be put to good use? Without his personal charisma, are we able the successfully carry out diplomatic work behind the scenes to secure or advance our national interests?

Looking ahead, despite many pressing challenges, I am cautiously optimistic that our generation of Singaporeans will pick up the mantle and respond effectively. It may well be that these involve repudiating or challenging some enduring beliefs, but Lee Kuan Yew himself would choose to do what is best for Singapore rather than what is dogmatically easy or expedient. That, perhaps, is the best way of honouring the legacy of our founding father. ❧

Dylan Loh is a Research Analyst at the S. Rajaratnam School of International Studies (RSIS), Nanyang Technological University, Singapore.

Contributors

ALAN CHONG

Alan Chong is an Associate Professor of International Relations at the S. Rajaratnam School of International Studies, Nanyang Technological University, Singapore.

ANG CHENG GUAN

Ang Cheng Guan is Head of Graduate Studies at the S. Rajaratnam School of International Studies (RSIS), Nanyang Technological University, Singapore.

ANG HWEE MIN

Ang Hwee Min is an Opinions Editor of the Nanyang Chronicle, a campus newspaper published by the Wee Kim Wee School of Communication and Information (WKWSCI), Nanyang Technological University, Singapore.

BARRY DESKER

Barry Desker is Distinguished Fellow at the S. Rajaratnam School of International Studies (RSIS), Nanyang Technological University, Singapore. He was Dean of RSIS and its predecessor Institute of Defence and Strategic Studies from 2000 to 2014. He was Singapore's ambassador to Indonesia from 1986 to 1993.

BILVEER SINGH

Bilveer Singh is an Associate Professor of Political Science at the National University of Singapore, and an Adjunct Senior Fellow at the Centre of Excellence for National Security (CENS), S. Rajaratnam School of International Studies (RSIS), Nanyang Technological University, Singapore.

BENJAMIN HO

Benjamin Ho is an Associate Research Fellow in the Multilateralism and Regionalism Programme, S. Rajaratnam School of International Studies (RSIS), Nanyang Technological University, Singapore.

CHAN HENG CHEE

Chan Heng Chee is a member of the Board of Governors of the S. Rajaratnam School of International Studies (RSIS), Nanyang Technological University, Singapore. She is also Ambassador-at-large and Chairman of the Lee Kuan Yew Centre for Innovative Cities at the Singapore University of Technology and Design (SUTD). She was a political science professor before becoming ambassador to the United States from 1996 to 2012.

C. RAJA MOHAN

C. Raja Mohan is a Distinguished Fellow at the Observer Research Foundation, New Delhi, and heads its strategic studies programme. He is an Adjunct Professor at the S. Rajaratnam School of International Studies (RSIS), Nanyang Technological University, Singapore, and a visiting research professor at the Institute of South Asian Studies (ISAS), National University of Singapore.

CHIA-YI LEE

Chia-yi Lee is an Assistant Professor at the S.Rajaratnam School of International Studies (RSIS), Nanyang Technological University, Singapore.

DANIEL CHUA

Daniel Chua is a Research Fellow at the Institute of Defence and Strategic Studies, S. Rajaratnam School of International Studies (RSIS), Nanyang Technological University, Singapore.

DAVID HAN

David Han is a Research Analyst with the Malaysia Programme at the S. Rajaratnam School of International Studies (RSIS), Nanyang Technological University, Singapore.

DYLAN LOH

Dylan Loh is a Research Analyst with the S. Rajaratnam School of International Studies (RSIS), Nanyang Technological University, Singapore.

EDDIE TEO

Eddie Teo is Chairman of the Board of Governors, S. Rajaratnam School of International Studies (RSIS), Nanyang Technological University, Singapore. He is also Chairman of the Public Service Commission who, as a public servant for 37 years, was Director, Security and Intelligence Division; Director, Internal Security Department; Permanent Secretary (Defence); and Permanent Secretary (Prime Minister's Office).

GREG MILLS

Greg Mills heads the Johannesburg-based Brenthurst Foundation. In 2014, he was a Senior Visiting Fellow at the S. Rajaratnam School of International Studies, Nanyang Technological University, Singapore.

HOO TIANG BOON

Hoo Tiang Boon is an Assistant Professor with the China Programme, and Coordinator of the MSc (Asian Studies) Programme at the S. Rajaratnam School of International Studies, Nanyang Technological University, Singapore.

JOSEPH CHINYONG LIOW

Joseph Chinyong Liow is Dean of the S. Rajaratnam School of International Studies (RSIS), Nanyang Technological University, Singapore. He is currently also Senior Fellow, Centre for East Asia Policy Studies, and the inaugural holder of the Lee Kuan Yew Chair in Southeast Asia Studies at The Brookings Institution.

JUSUF WANANDI

Jusuf Wanandi is a Vice Chairman on the Board of Trustees at the CSIS Foundation in Jakarta, and a founding director of The Jakarta Post.

KEVIN YL TAN

Kevin YL Tan is an Adjunct Professor at the S. Rajaratnam School of International Studies (RSIS), Nanyang Technological University, Singapore and at the Faculty of Law, National University of Singapore. He is the editor and author of over 30 books on the law, history and politics of Singapore.

KUMAR RAMAKRISHNA

Kumar Ramakrishna is an Associate Professor and Head of Policy Studies in the Office of the Executive Deputy Chairman, S. Rajaratnam School of International Studies (RSIS), Nanyang Technological University, Singapore.

LO YI MIN

Lo Yi Min is an Opinions Editor of the Nanyang Chronicle, a campus newspaper published by the Wee Kim Wee School of Communication and Information (WKWSCI), Nanyang Technological University, Singapore.

MUSHAHID ALI

Mushahid Ali is a Senior Fellow with the S. Rajaratnam School of International Studies (RSIS), Nanyang Technological University, Singapore.

NUR DIYANAH ANWAR

Nur Diyanah Anwar is a Research Analyst with the Centre of Excellence for National Security (CENS) at the S. Rajaratnam School of International Studies (RSIS), Nanyang Technological University, Singapore.

ONG KENG YONG

Ong Keng Yong is Executive Deputy Chairman of the S. Rajaratnam School of International Studies (RSIS), Nanyang Technological University, Singapore.

PRADUMNA B. RANA

Pradumna B. Rana is an Associate Professor and Coordinator of the International Political Economy Programme, Nanyang Technological University, Singapore.

TOH TING WEI

Toh Ting Wei was, until recently, the News Editor of the Nanyang Chronicle, a campus newspaper published by the Wee Kim Wee School of Communication and Information (WKWSCI), at the Nanyang Technological University, Singapore.

WANG GUNGWU

Wang Gungwu is University Professor of the National University of Singapore, Chairman of the East Asian Institute, and former member of the Board of Governors of the S. Rajaratnam School of International Studies (RSIS), Nanyang Technological University, Singapore.

YANG RAZALI KASSIM

Yang Razali Kassim is a Senior Fellow with the S. Rajaratnam School of International Studies (RSIS), Nanyang Technological University, Singapore, where he is also Editor of RSIS Commentary and Editor of Strategic Currents.

ZHA DAOJIONG

Zha Daojiong is a Professor of International Political Economy, School of International Studies, Peking University. He was a Visiting Senior Fellow in 2009 and 2011 at the S. Rajaratnam School of International Studies (RSIS), Nanyang Technological University, Singapore.

About the Editors

YANG RAZALI KASSIM is Senior Fellow with the S. Rajaratnam School of International Studies (RSIS), Nanyang Technological University. He is also Editor of *RSIS Commentary; Strategic Currents; and Reflections: Legacy of Lee Kuan Yew.*

MUSHAHID ALI is Senior Fellow with the S. Rajaratnam School of International Studies (RSIS), Nanyang Technological University. He is Co-editor of *Reflections: Legacy of Lee Kuan Yew.*

About RSIS

The S. Rajaratnam School of International Studies (RSIS) was inaugurated in January 2007 as an autonomous School within the Nanyang Technological University (NTU), upgraded from its previous incarnation as the Institute of Defence and Strategic Studies (IDSS), which was established in 1996.

The School exists to develop a community of scholars and policy analysts at the forefront of the Asia-Pacific security studies and international affairs. Its three core functions are related to research, graduate teaching and networking activities in the Asia-Pacific region. It produces cutting-edge security related research in Asia-Pacific Security, Conflict and Non-Traditional Security, International Political Economy, and Country and Area Studies.

The School's activities are aimed at assisting policymakers to develop comprehensive approaches to strategic thinking on issues related to security and stability in the Asia-Pacific and their implications for Singapore. The faculty and research staff at the School consists of local and international specialists in the fields of strategic studies, terrorism studies, international relations, international political economy, foreign policy analysis and defence technology.